PHAIDON

This diary belongs to

....

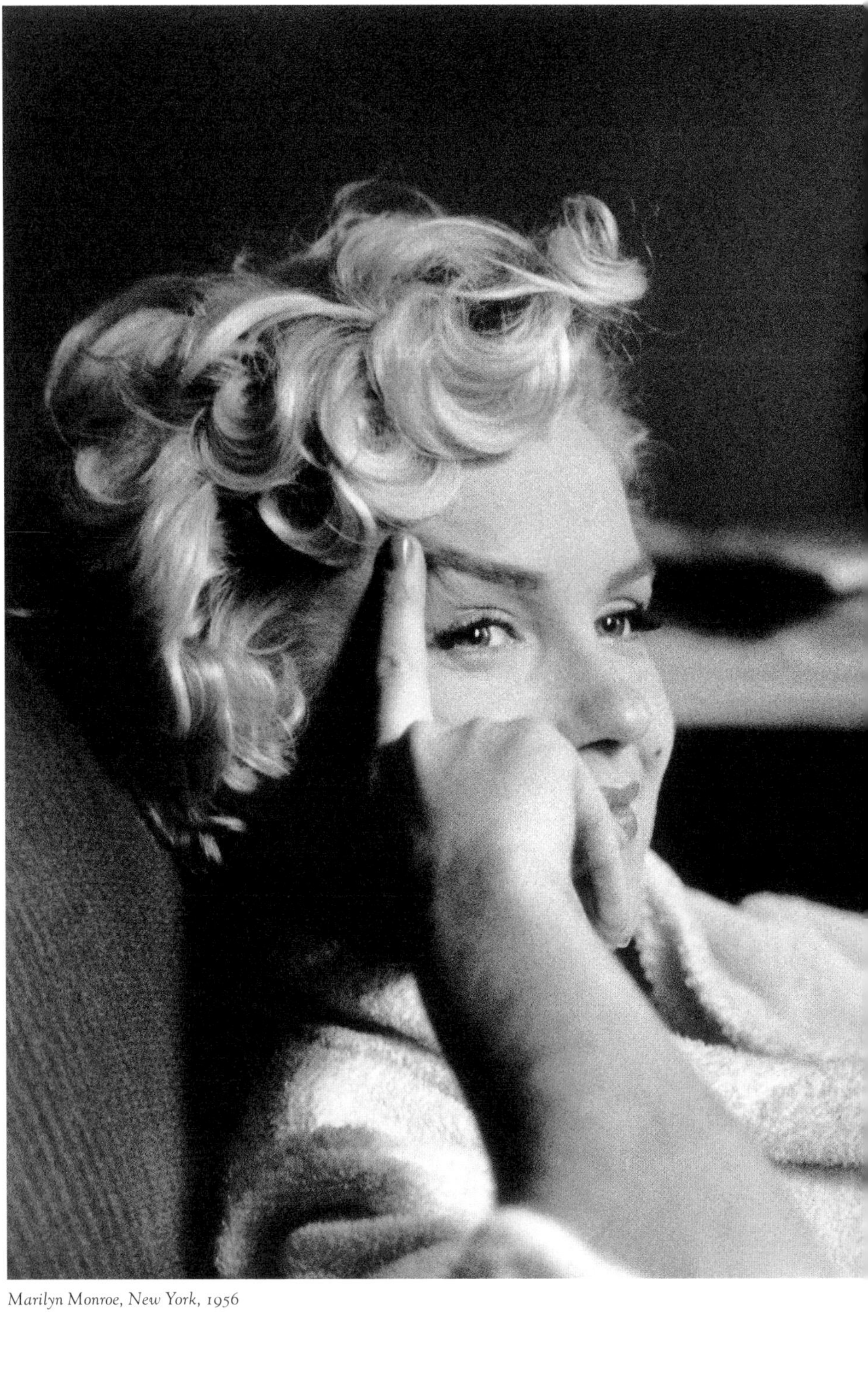

Marilyn Monroe, New York, 1956

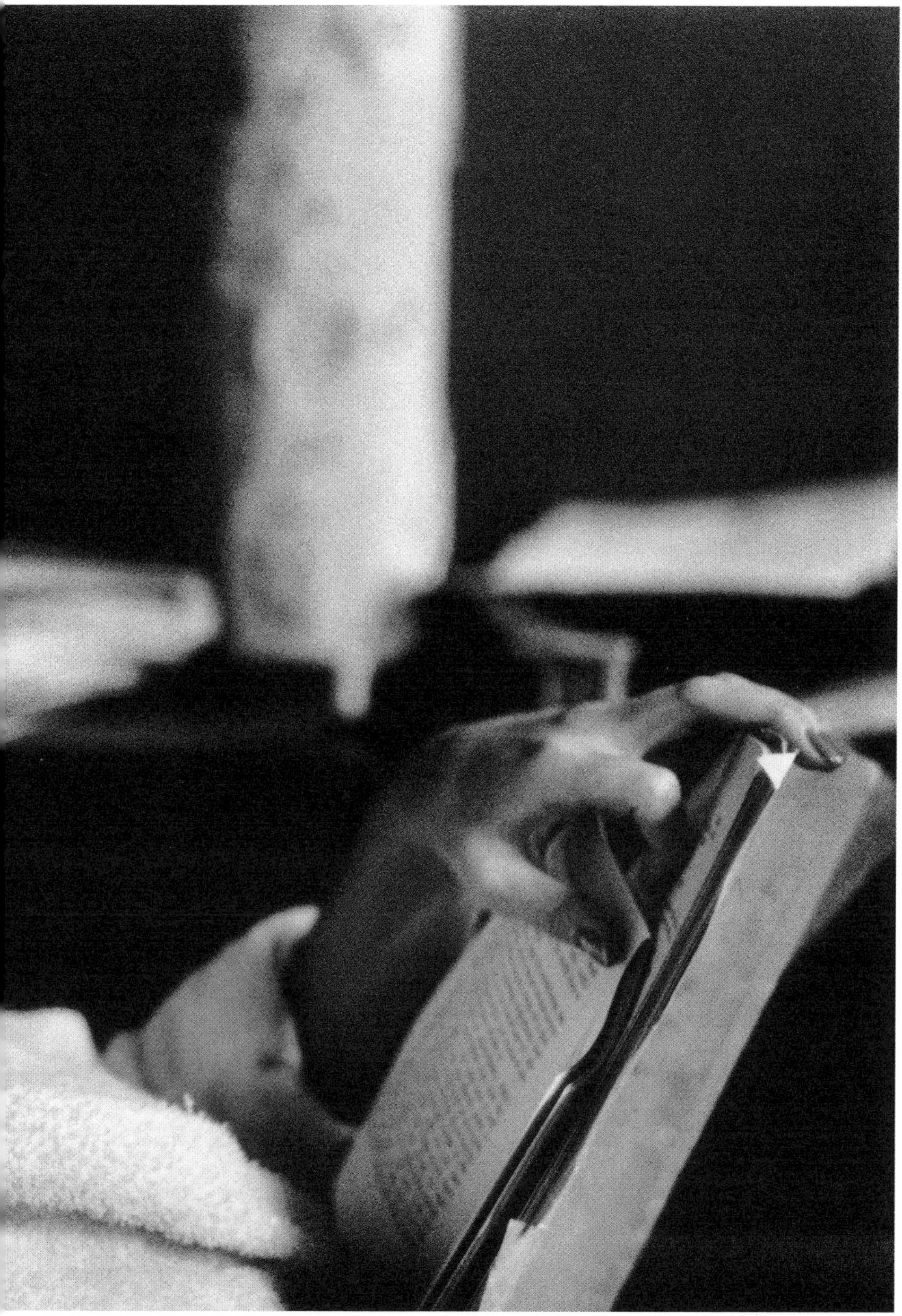

31 *Monday*

1 *Tuesday* Holiday

2 *Wednesday* Holiday (Scotland, New Zealand)

3 *Thursday*

4 *Friday*

5 *Saturday*

6 *Sunday*

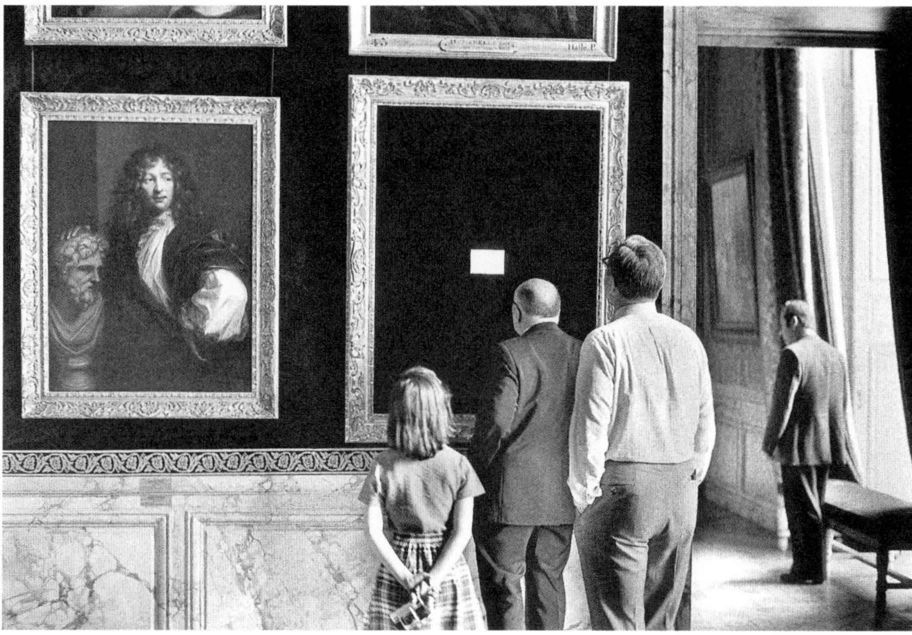

Versailles, France, 1975

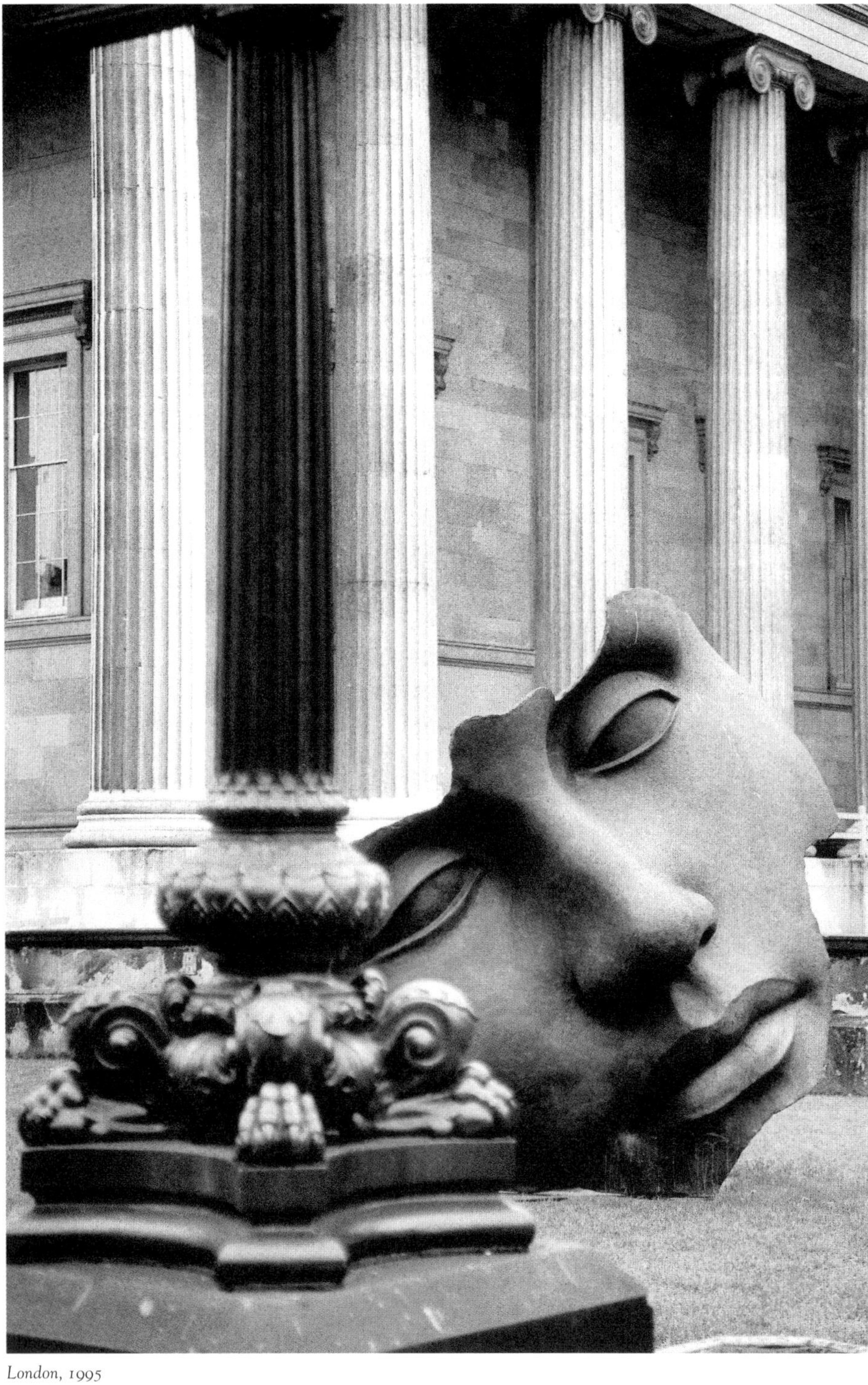

London, 1995

7 *Monday*

8 *Tuesday*

9 *Wednesday*

10 *Thursday*

11 *Friday*

12 *Saturday*

13 *Sunday*

14 *Monday*

15 *Tuesday*

16 *Wednesday*

17 *Thursday*

18 *Friday*

19 *Saturday*

20 *Sunday*

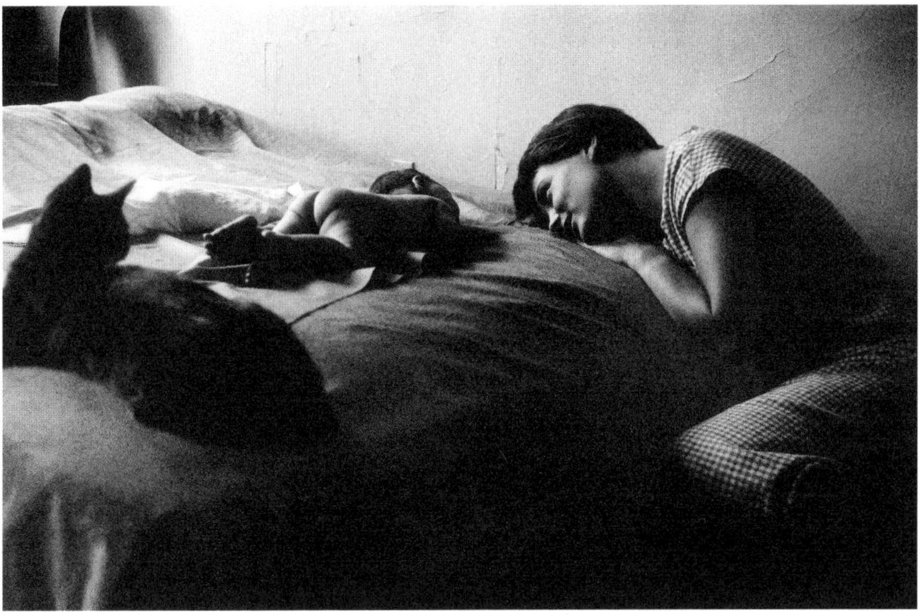

New York, 1953

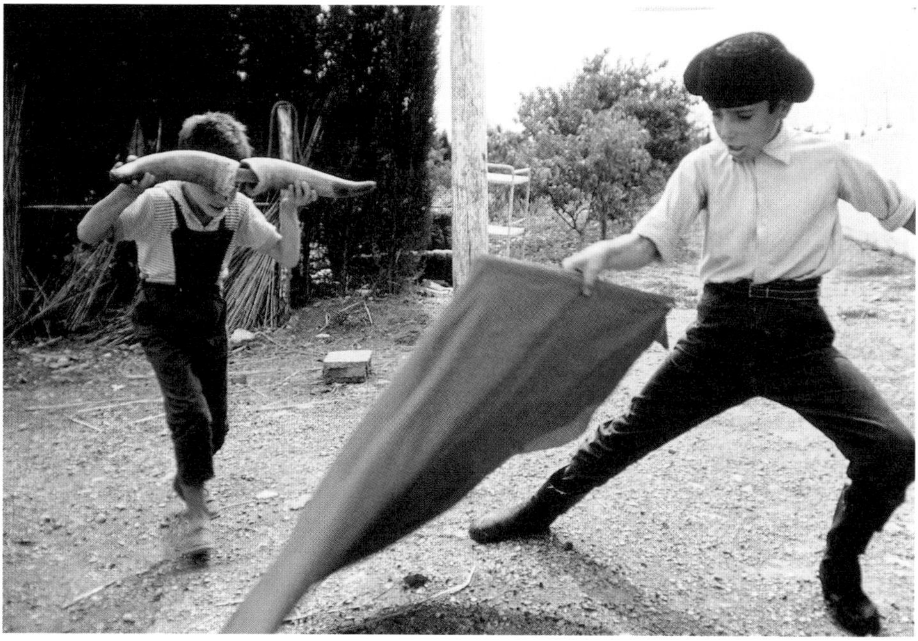

Southern Spain, 1969

21 Monday

Holiday (USA)

22 Tuesday

23 Wednesday

24 Thursday

25 Friday

26 Saturday

27 Sunday

28 Monday

29 Tuesday

30 Wednesday

31 Thursday

1 Friday

2 Saturday

3 Sunday

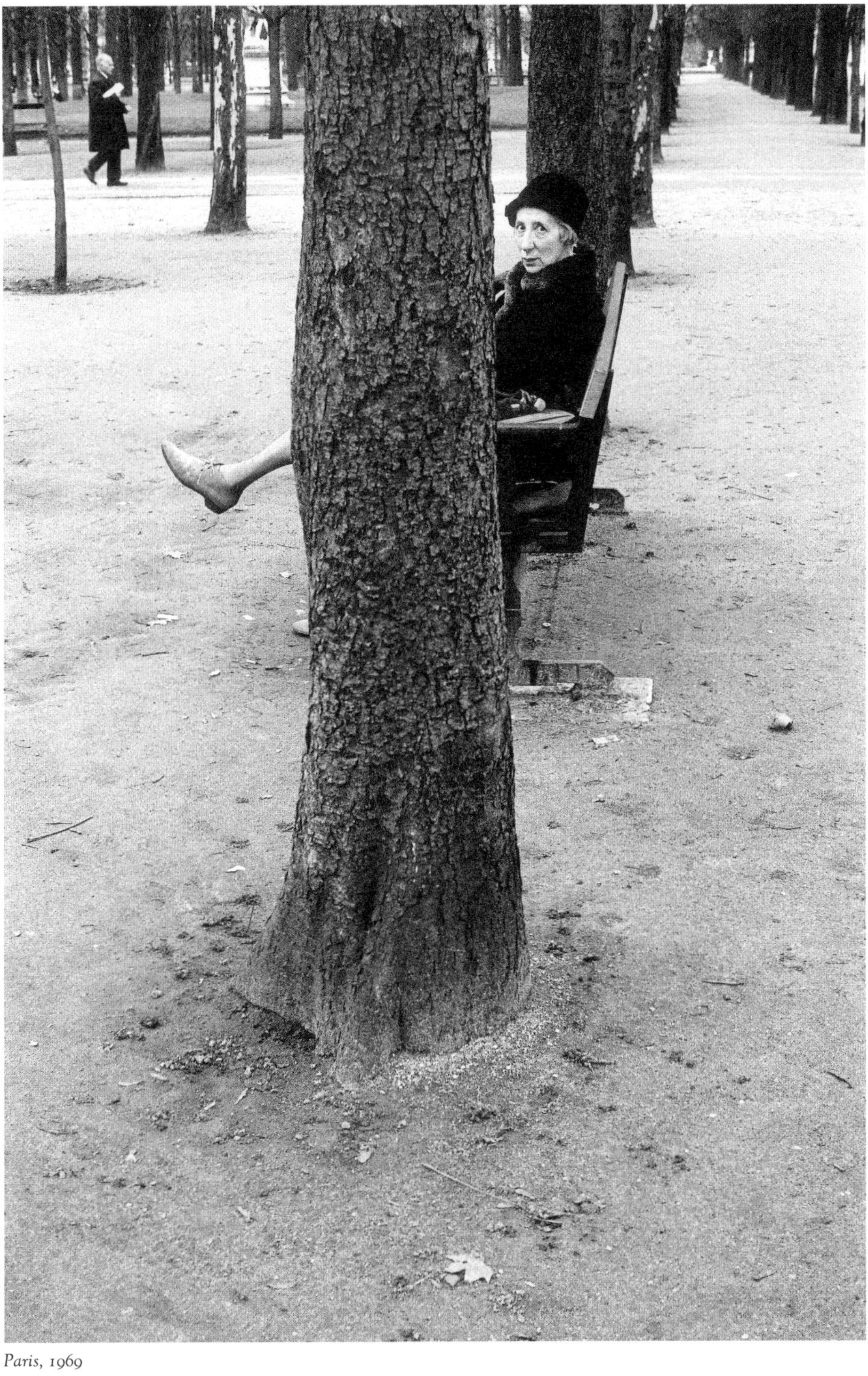

Paris, 1969

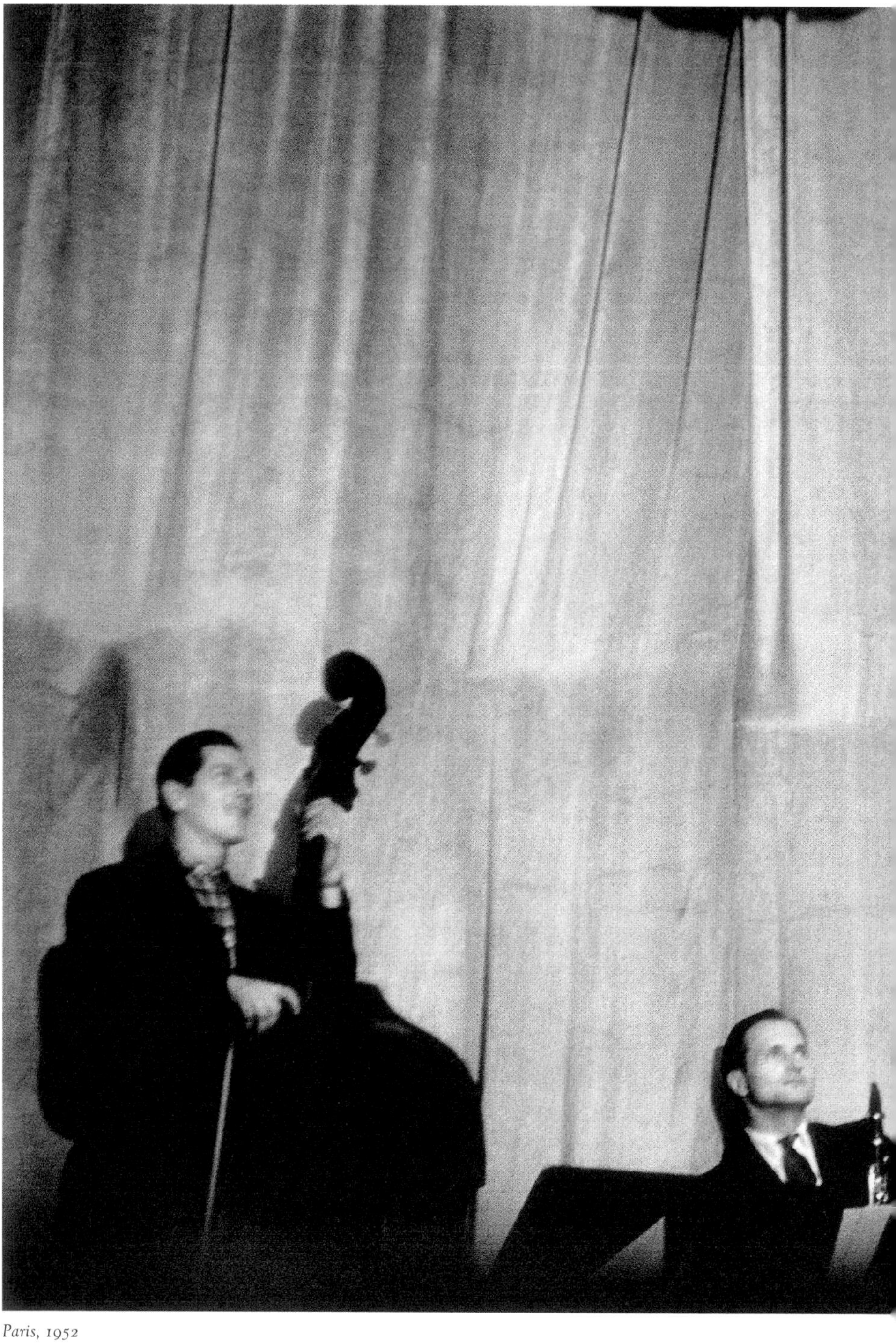

Paris, 1952

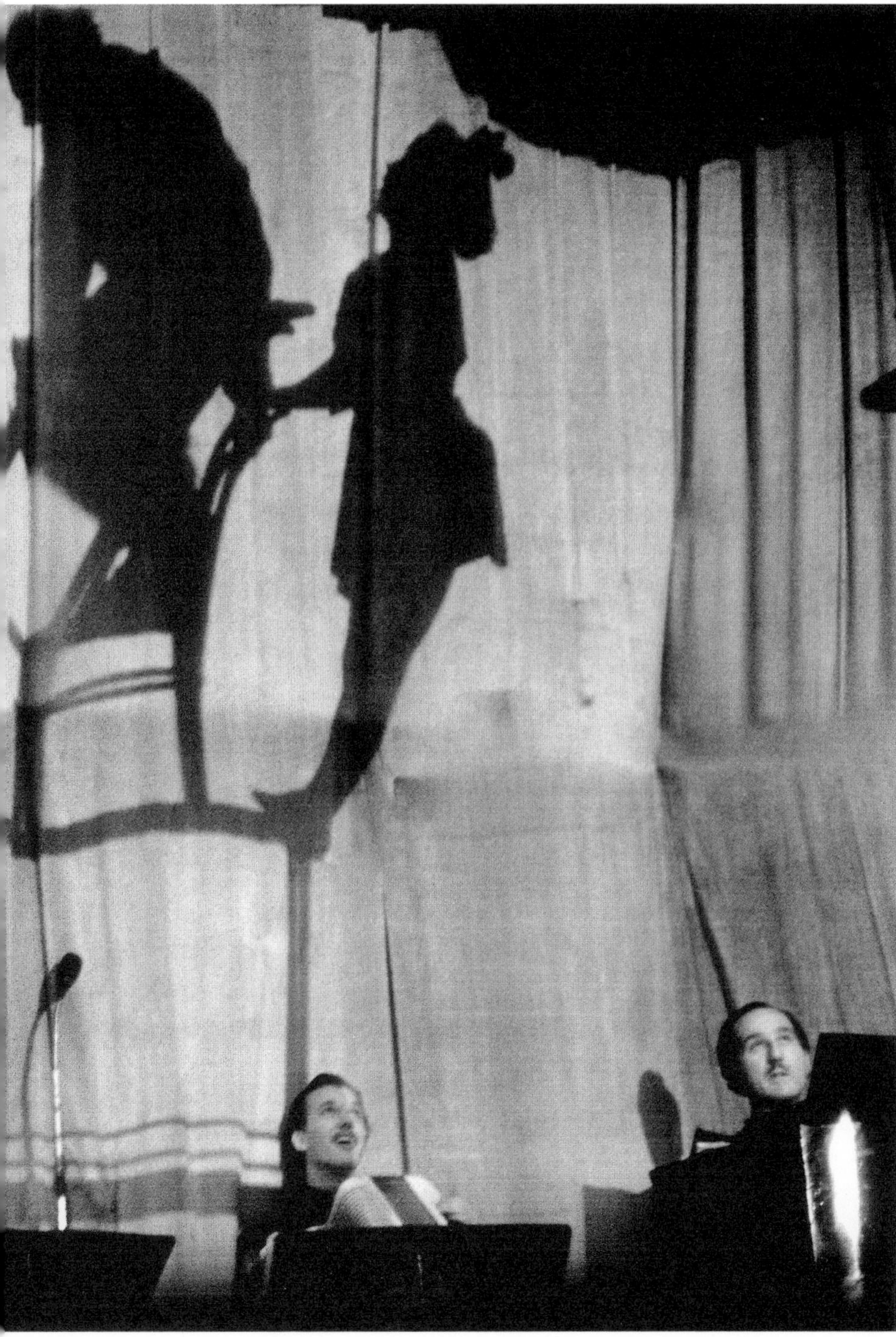

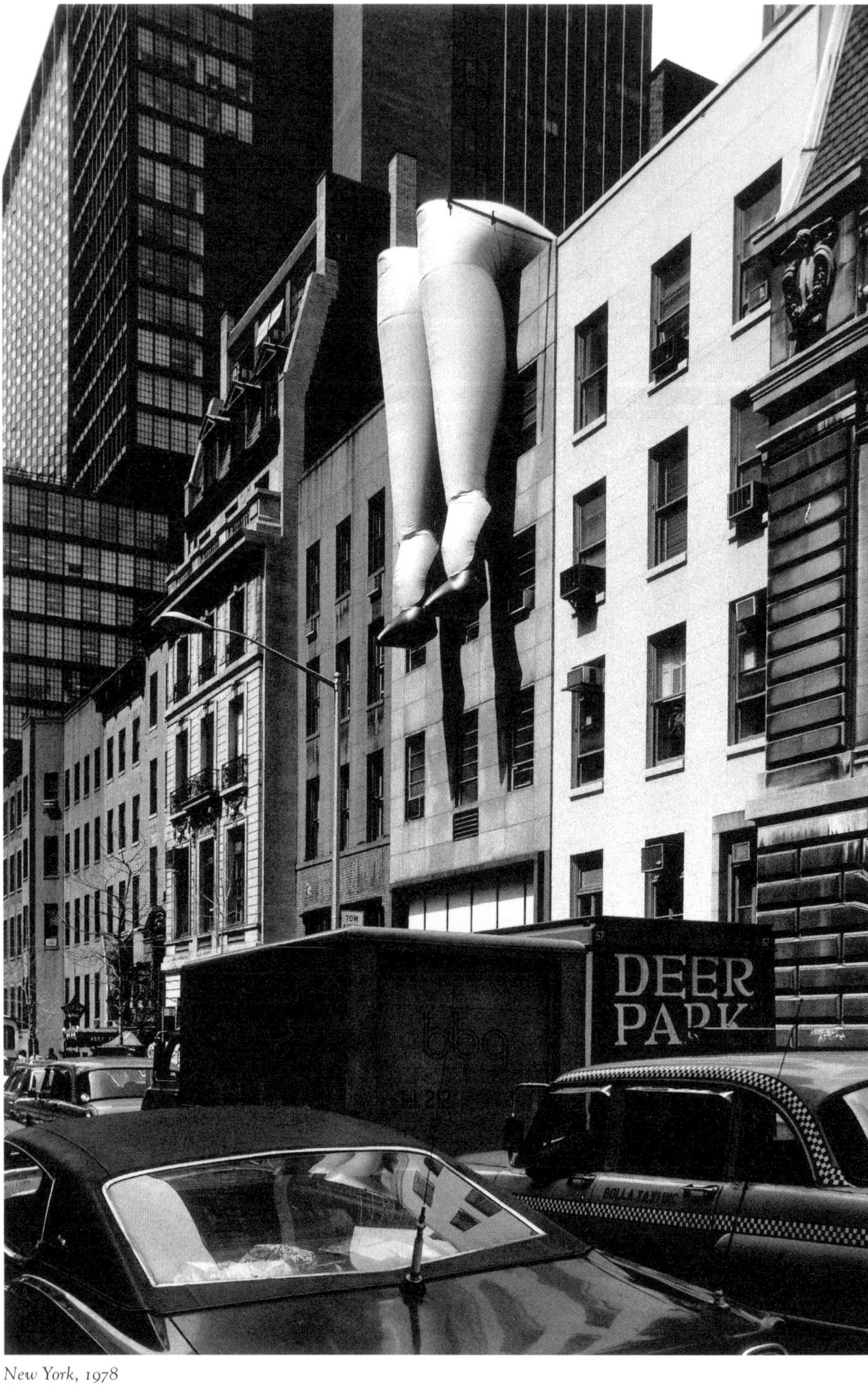

New York, 1978

4 *Monday*

5 *Tuesday*

6 *Wednesday*

Holiday (New Zealand)

7 *Thursday*

8 *Friday*

9 *Saturday*

10 *Sunday*

11 *Monday*

12 *Tuesday*

13 *Wednesday*

14 *Thursday*

15 *Friday*

16 *Saturday*

17 *Sunday*

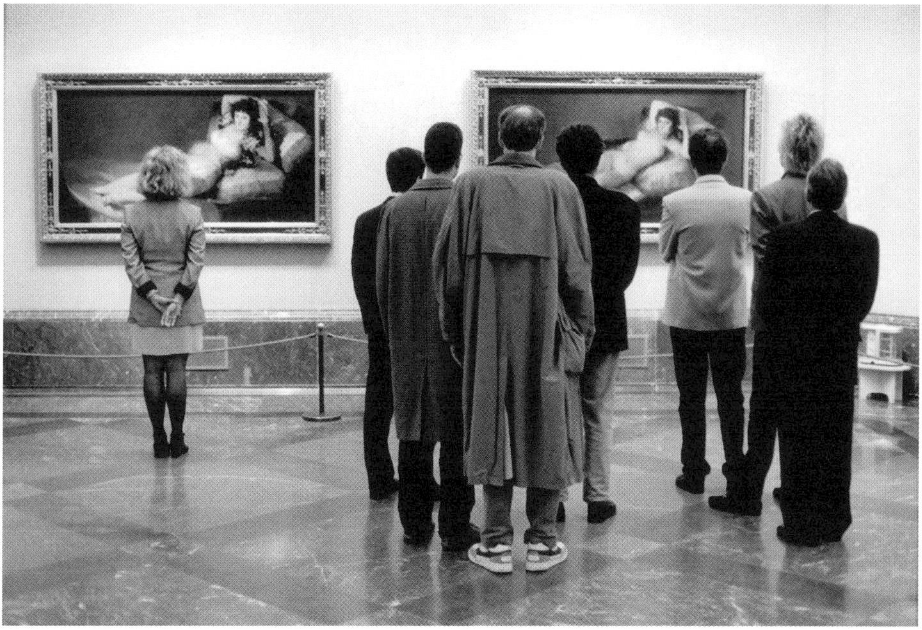

Museo del Prado, Madrid, 1995

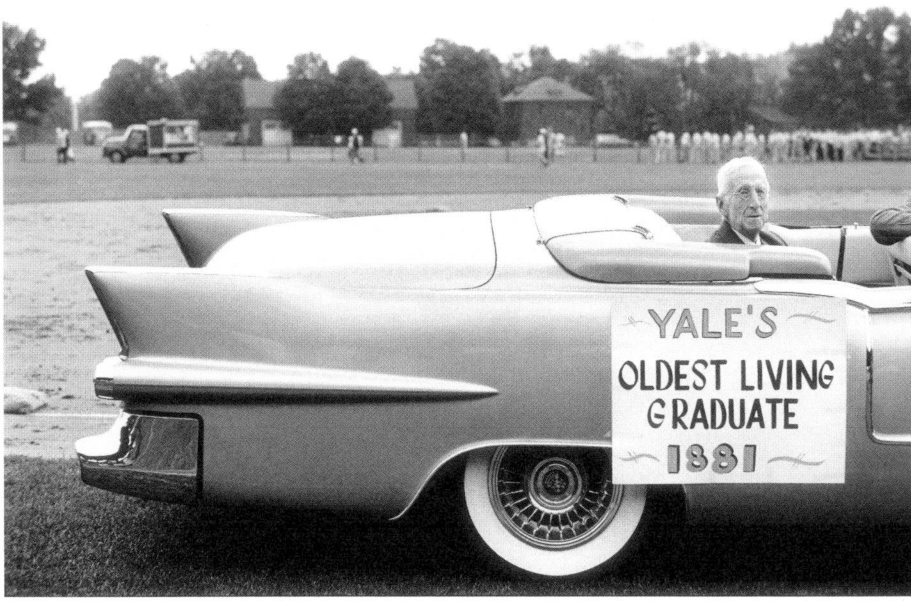

New Haven, Connecticut, 1955

February 2008

18 *Monday* Holiday (USA)

19 *Tuesday*

20 *Wednesday*

21 *Thursday*

22 *Friday*

23 *Saturday*

24 *Sunday*

25 *Monday*

26 *Tuesday*

27 *Wednesday*

28 *Thursday*

29 *Friday*

1 *Saturday*

2 *Sunday*

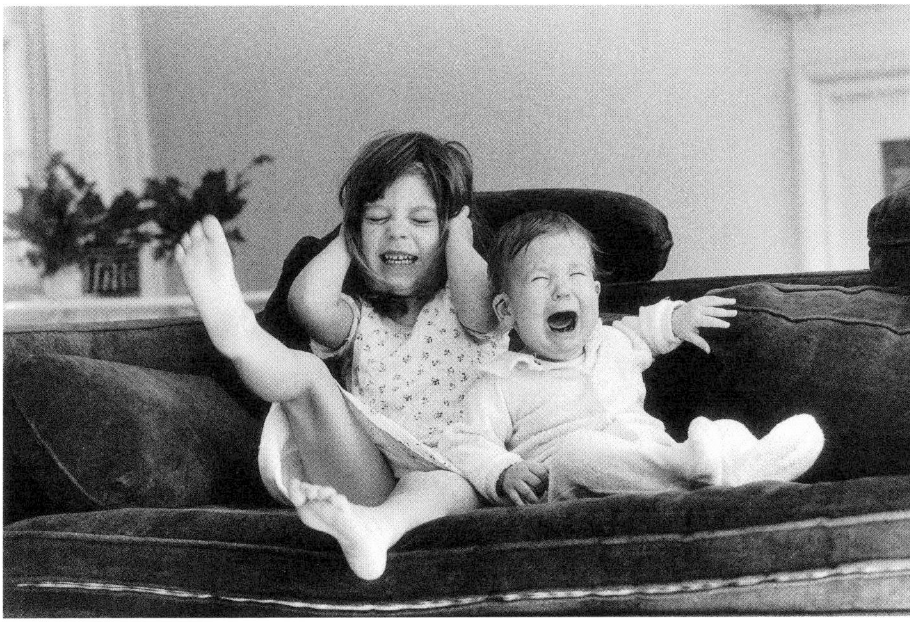

East Hampton, New York, 1981

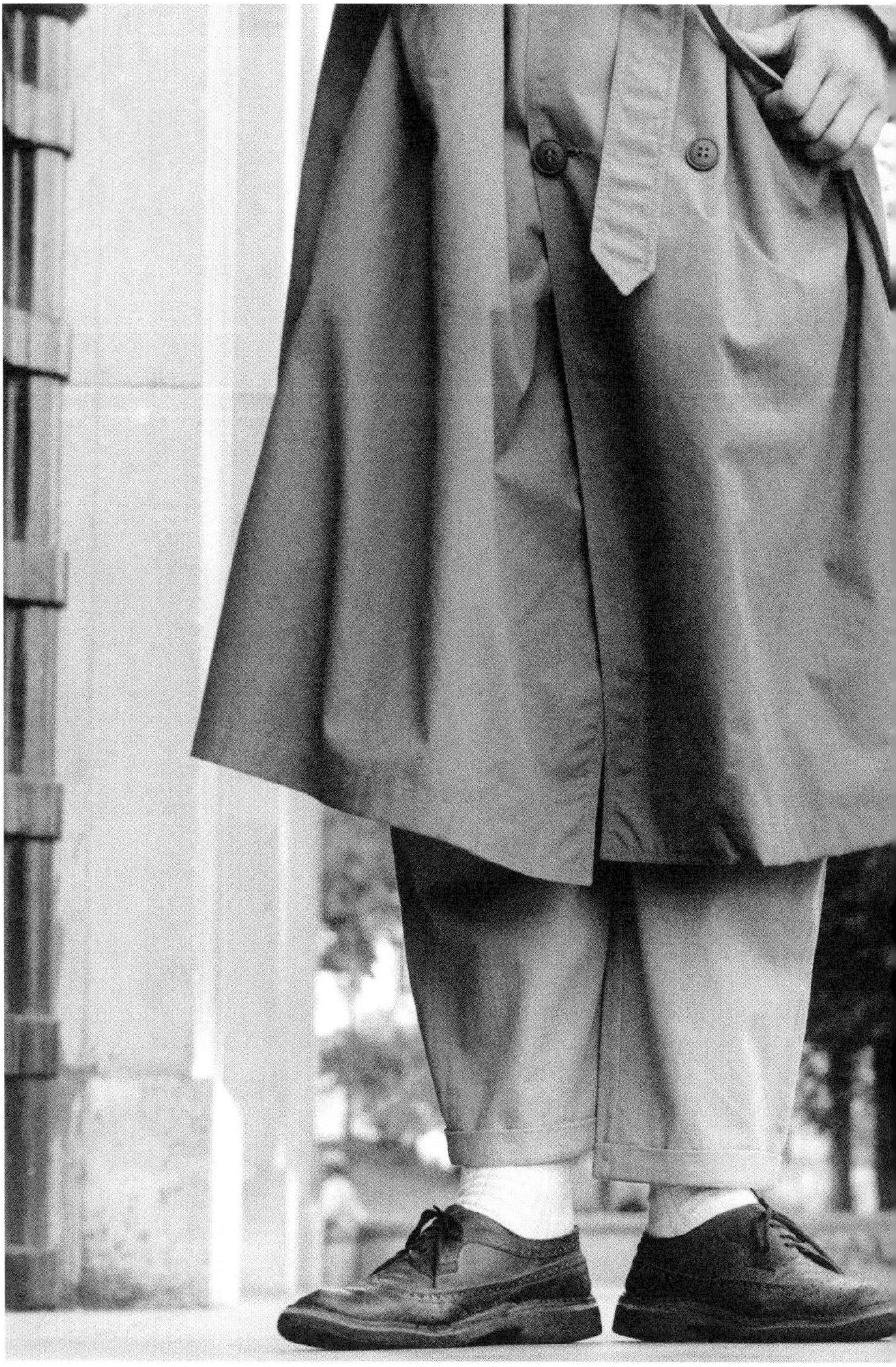

Paris, 1989

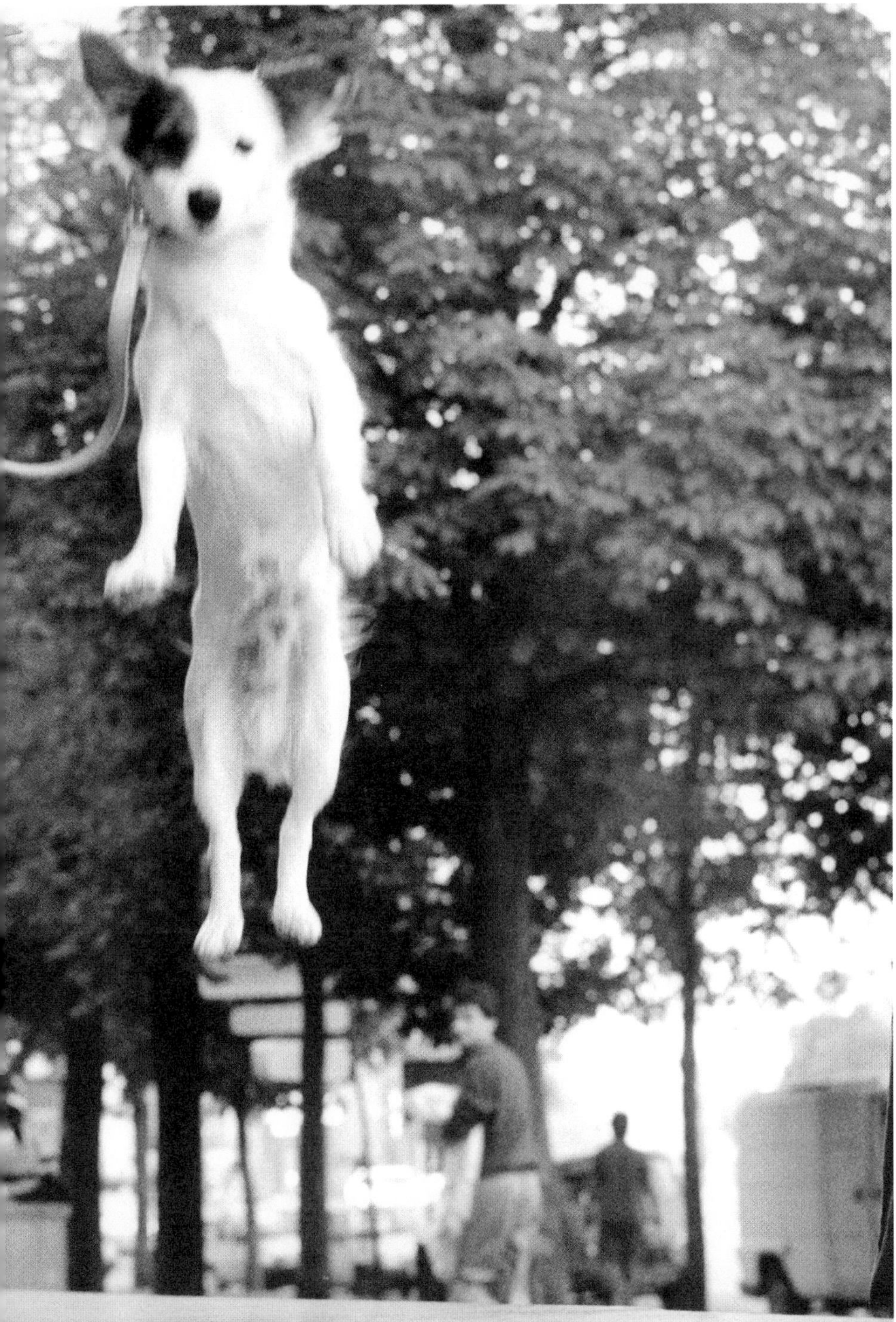

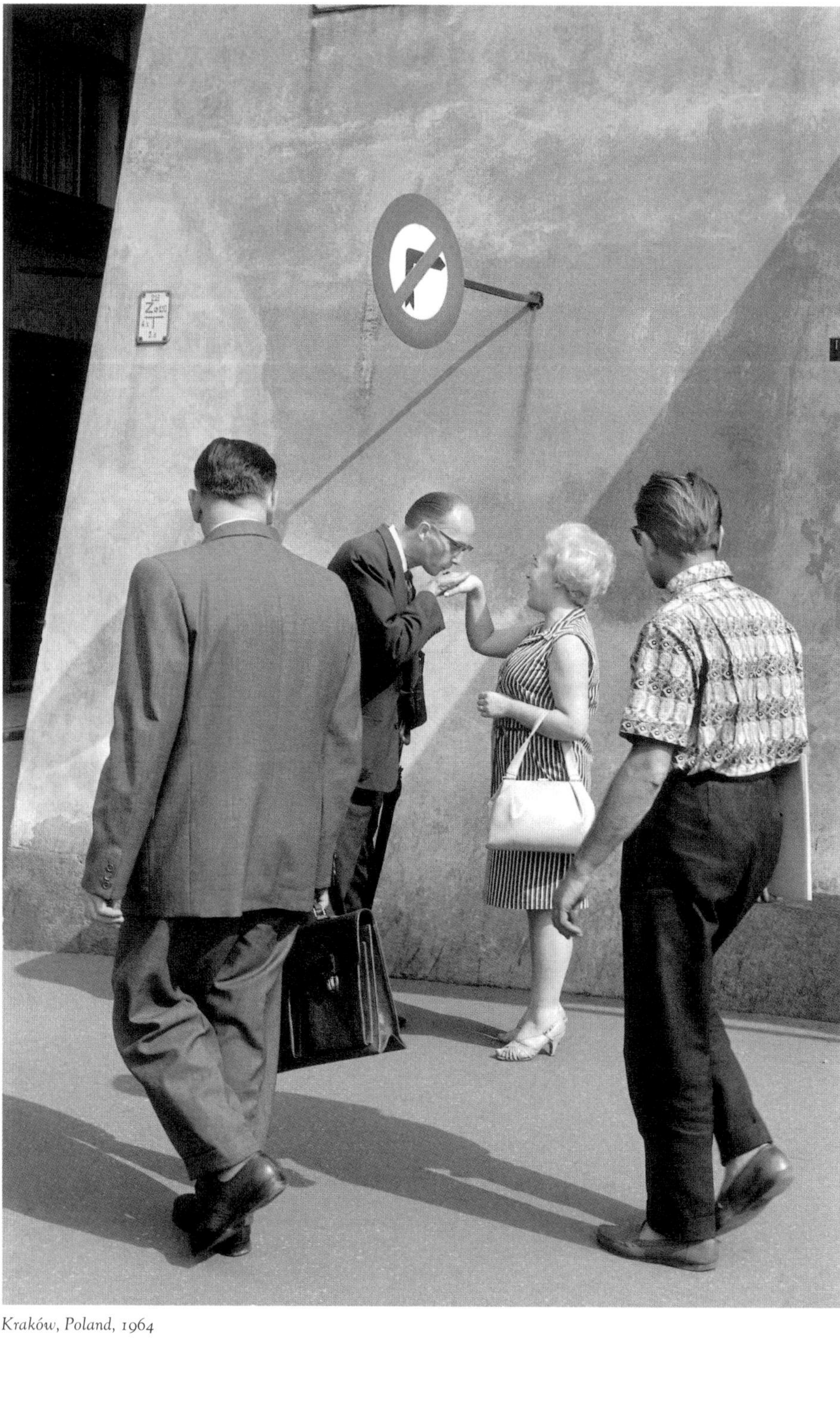

Kraków, Poland, 1964

March 2008

3 Monday

4 Tuesday

5 Wednesday

6 Thursday

7 Friday

8 Saturday

9 Sunday

10 Monday

11 Tuesday

12 Wednesday

13 Thursday

14 Friday

15 Saturday

16 Sunday

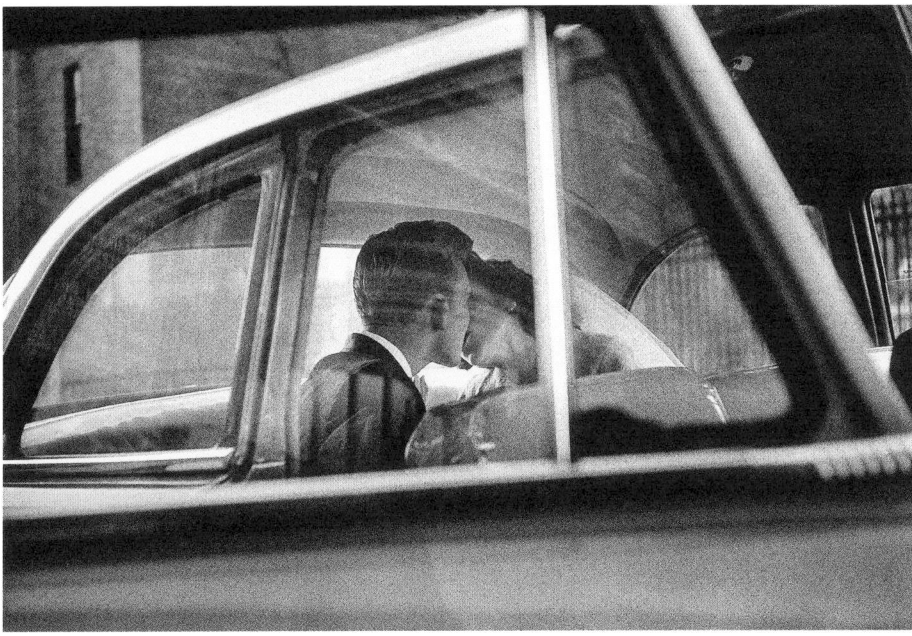

New York, 1955

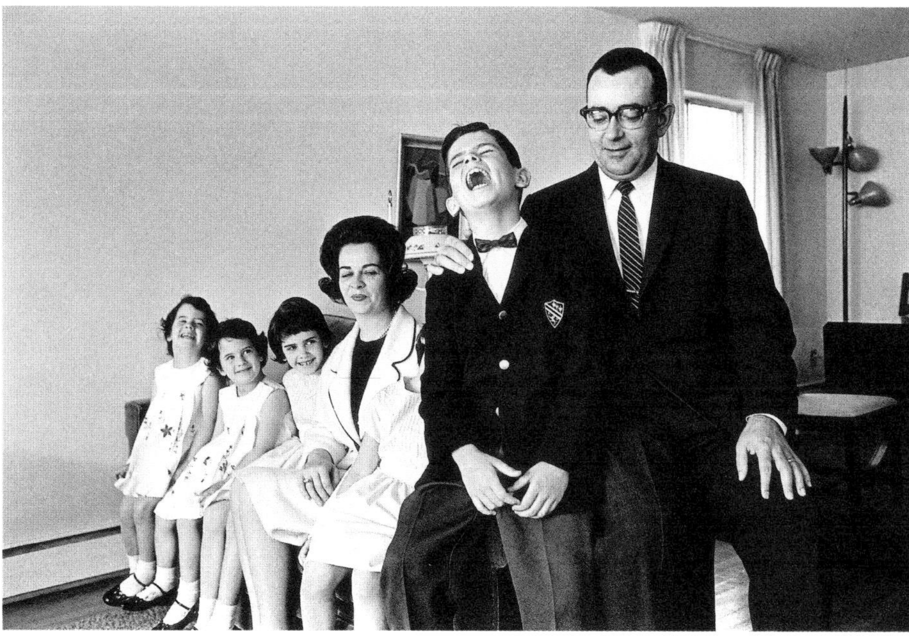

USA, 1963

17 *Monday*

Holiday
(N Ireland)

18 *Tuesday*

19 *Wednesday*

20 *Thursday*

21 *Friday*

Holiday
(UK, Australia, Canada, New Zealand)

22 *Saturday*

23 *Sunday*

24 Monday

Holiday
(UK except Scotland, Australia, Canada, New Zealand)

25 *Tuesday*

26 *Wednesday*

27 *Thursday*

28 *Friday*

29 *Saturday*

30 *Sunday*

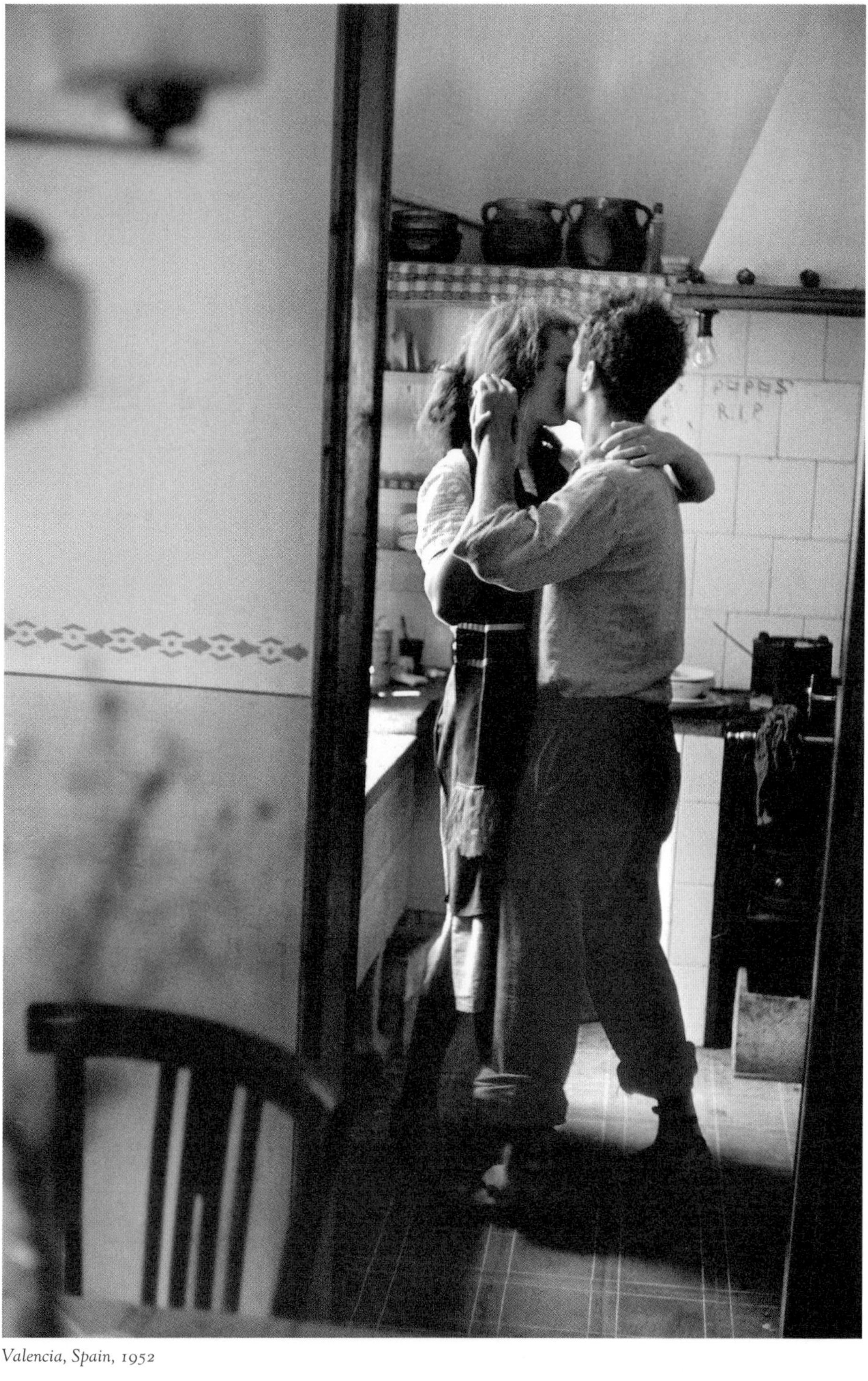

Valencia, Spain, 1952

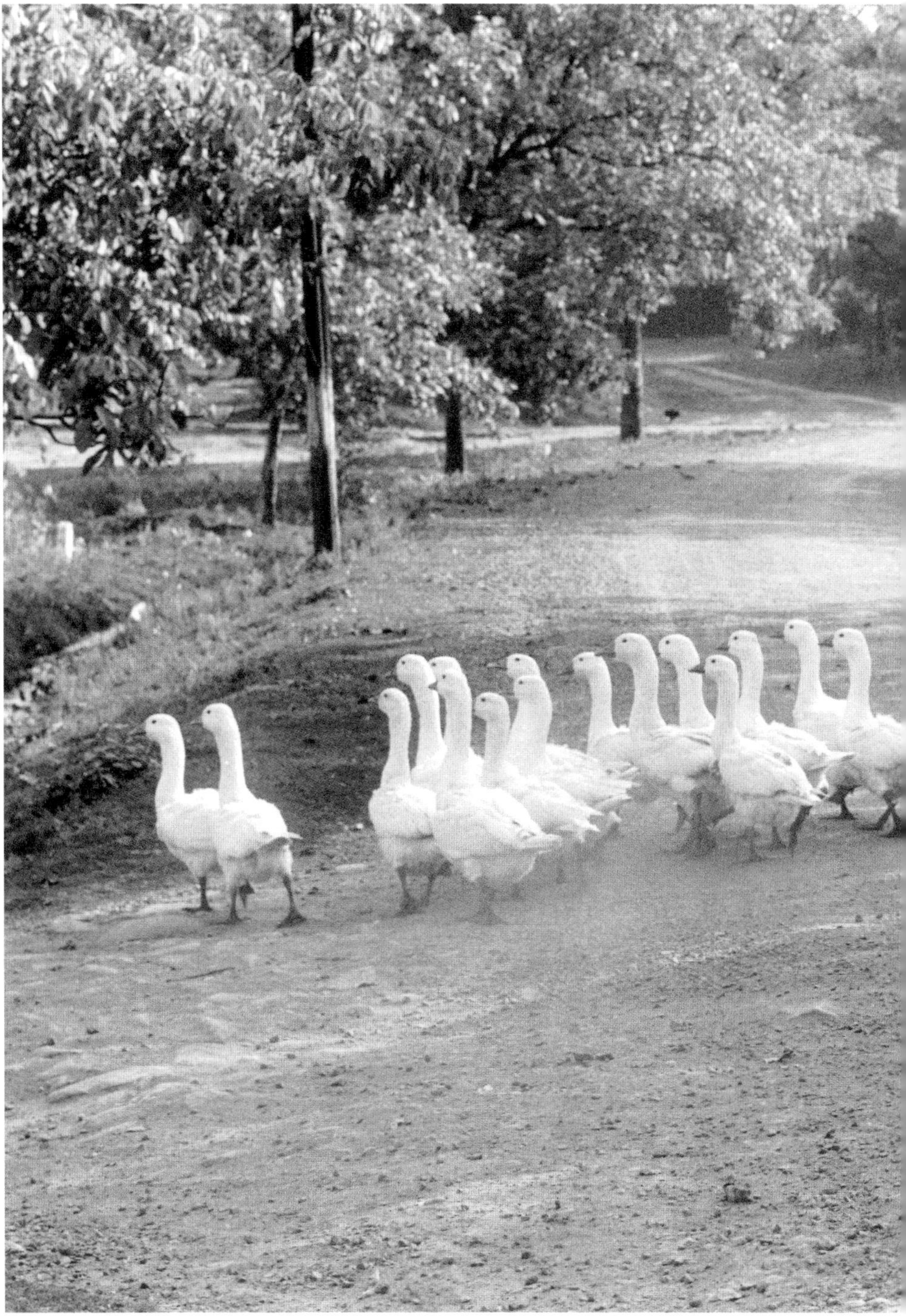
Hungary, 1964

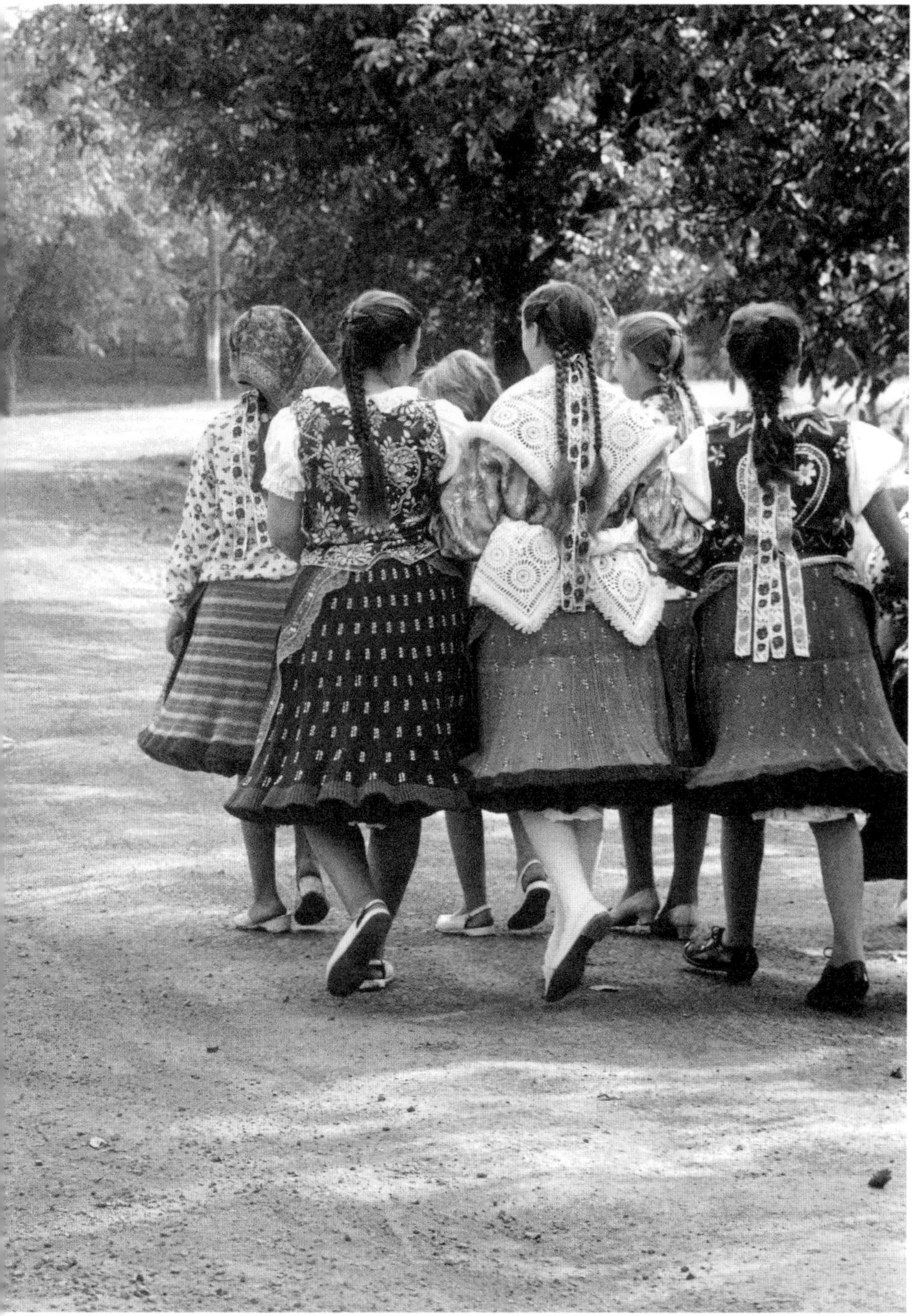

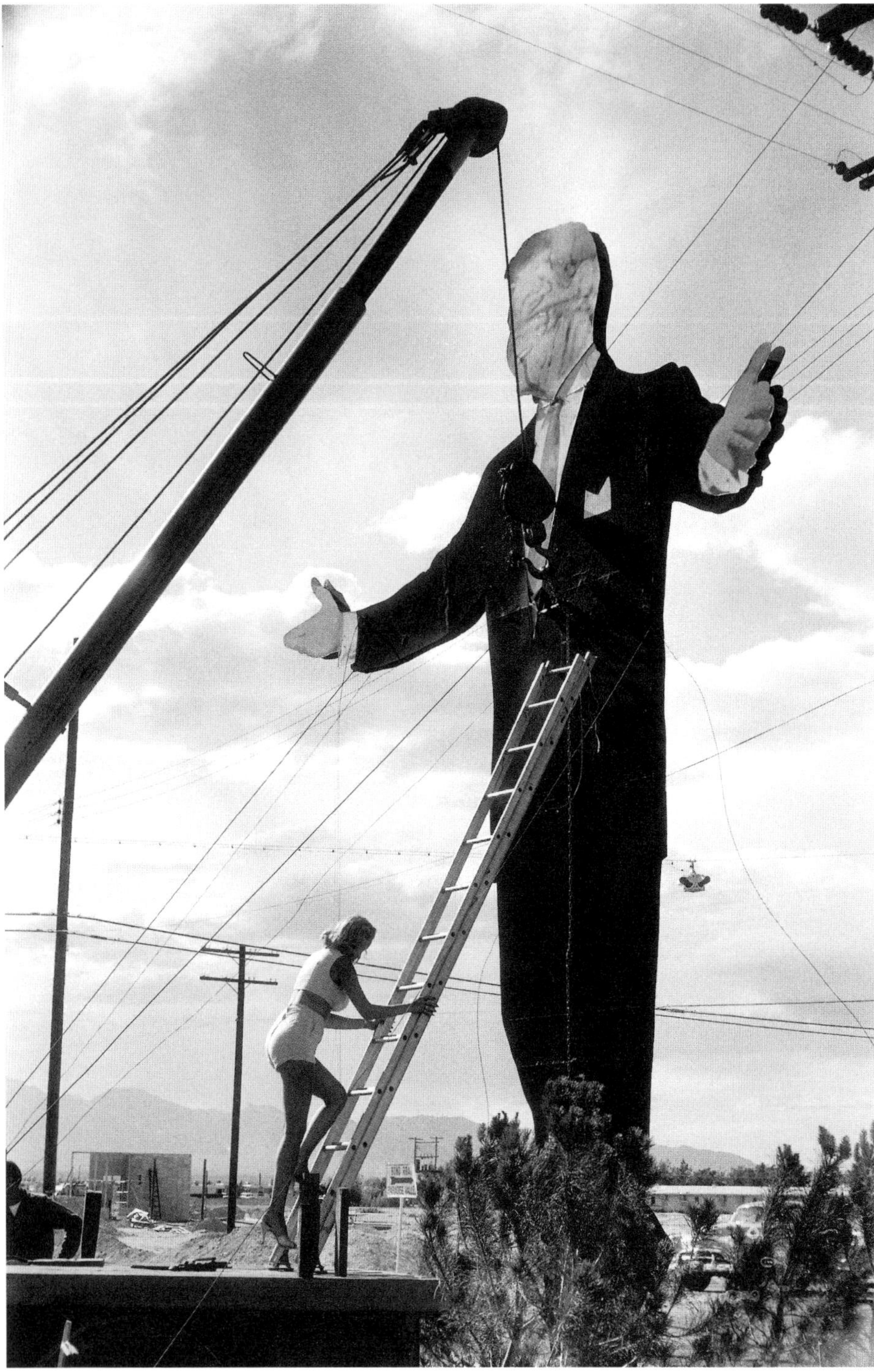

Las Vegas, 1957

31 *Monday*

1 *Tuesday*

2 *Wednesday*

3 *Thursday*

4 *Friday*

5 *Saturday*

6 *Sunday*

7 *Monday*

8 *Tuesday*

9 *Wednesday*

10 *Thursday*

11 *Friday*

12 *Saturday*

13 *Sunday*

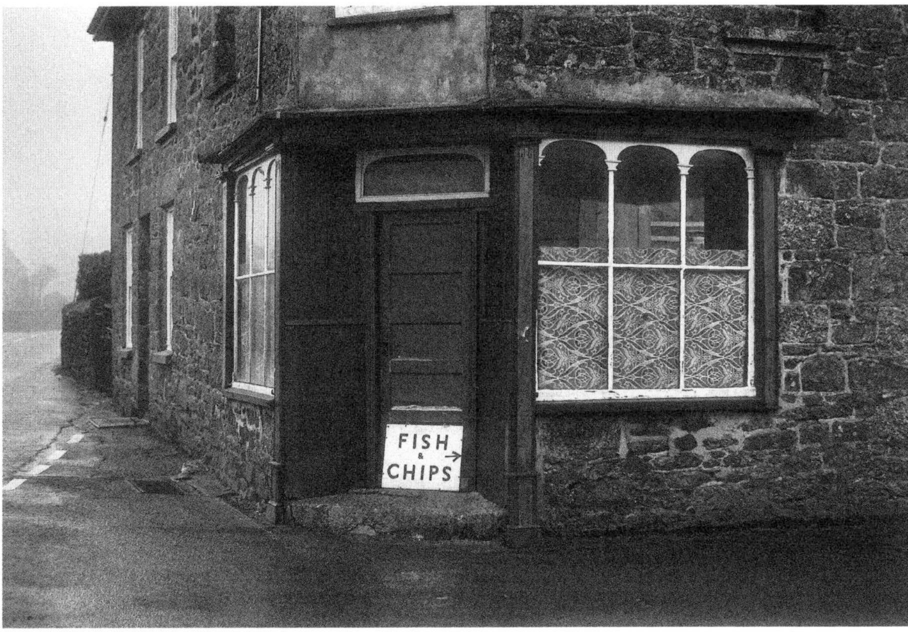

Land's End, Cornwall, England, 1971

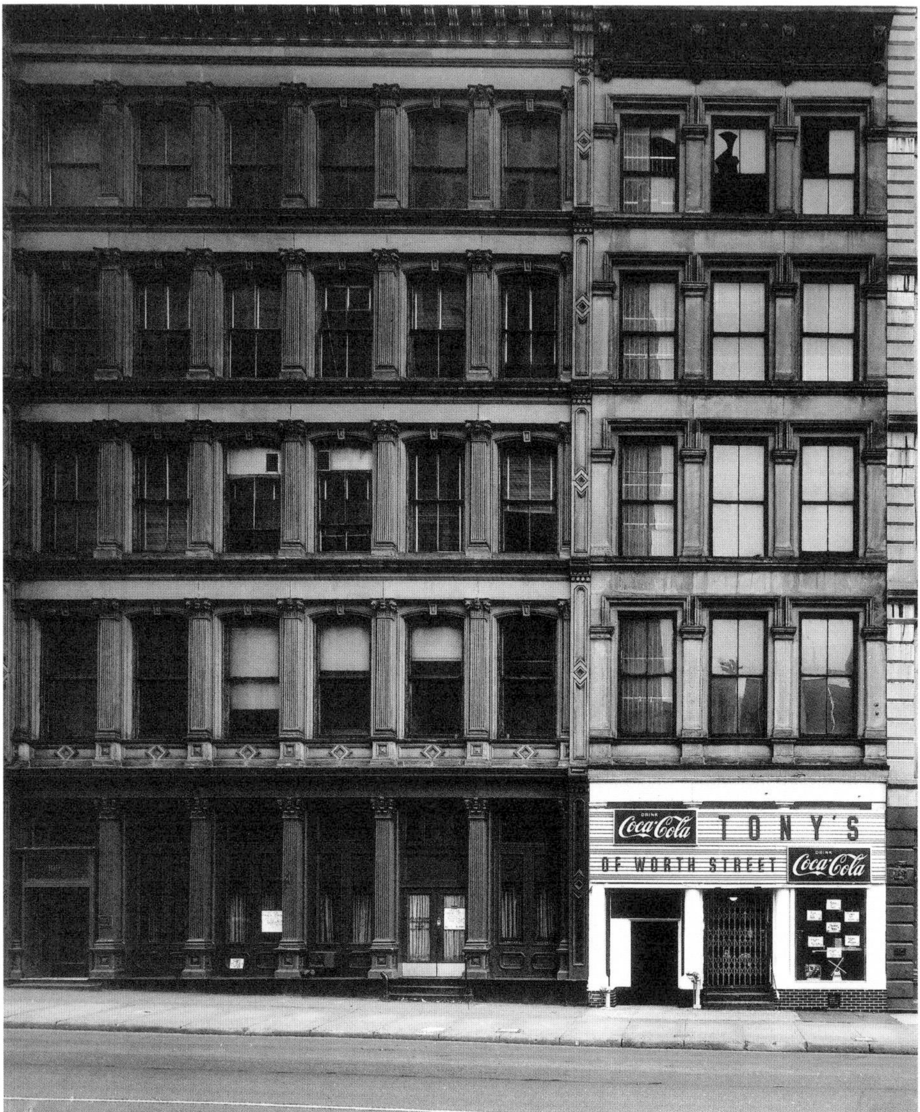

New York, 1969

14 Monday

15 Tuesday

16 Wednesday

17 Thursday

18 Friday

19 Saturday

20 Sunday

21 *Monday*

22 *Tuesday*

23 *Wednesday*

24 *Thursday*

25 *Friday*

Holiday
(Australia, New Zealand)

26 *Saturday*

27 *Sunday*

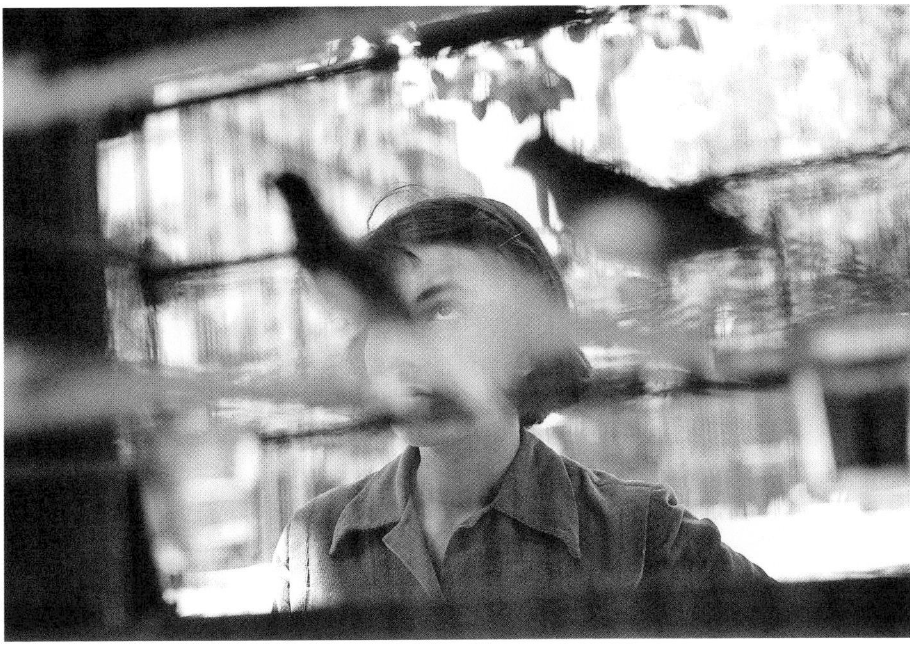

Paris, 1949

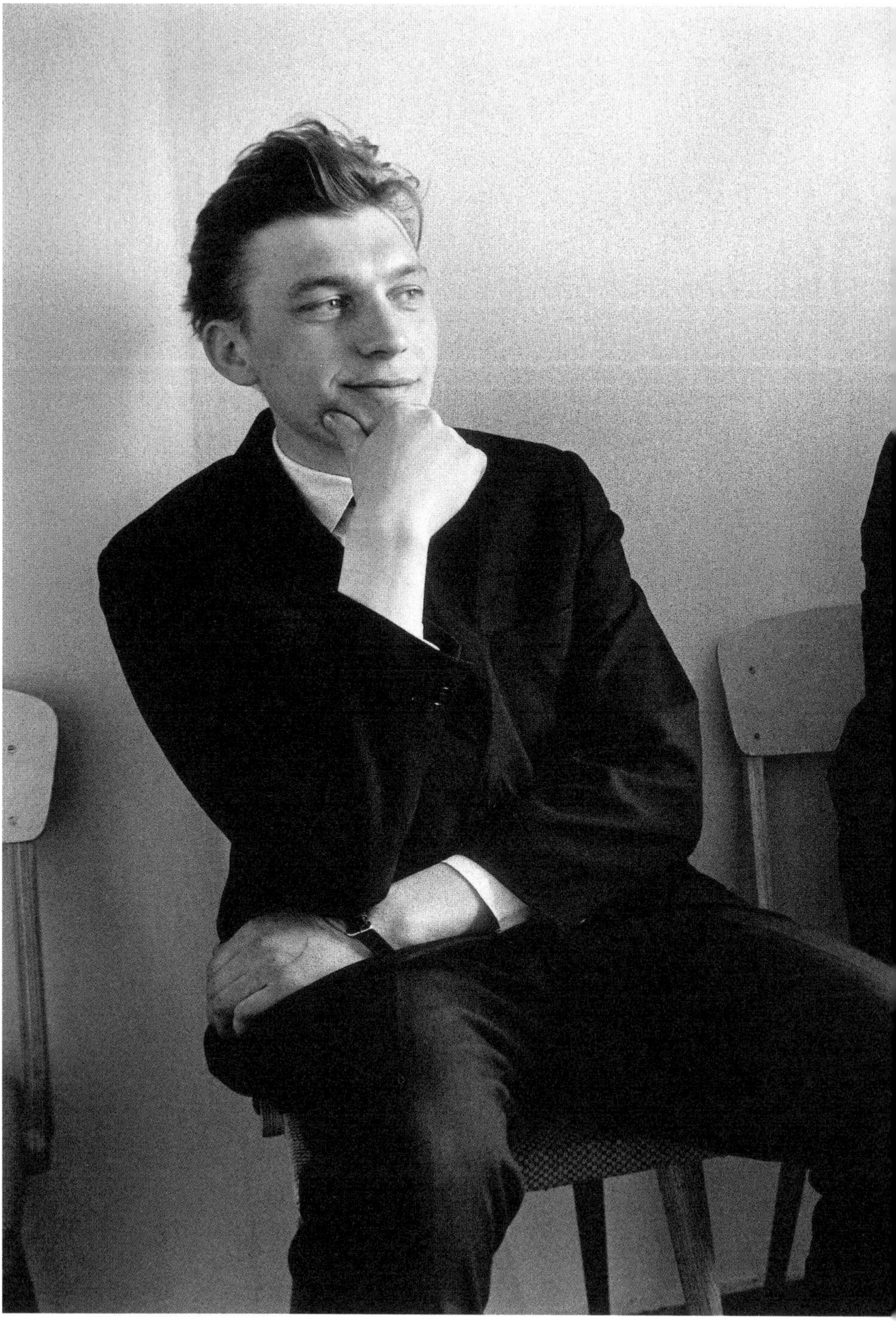

Bratsk, Siberia, 1967

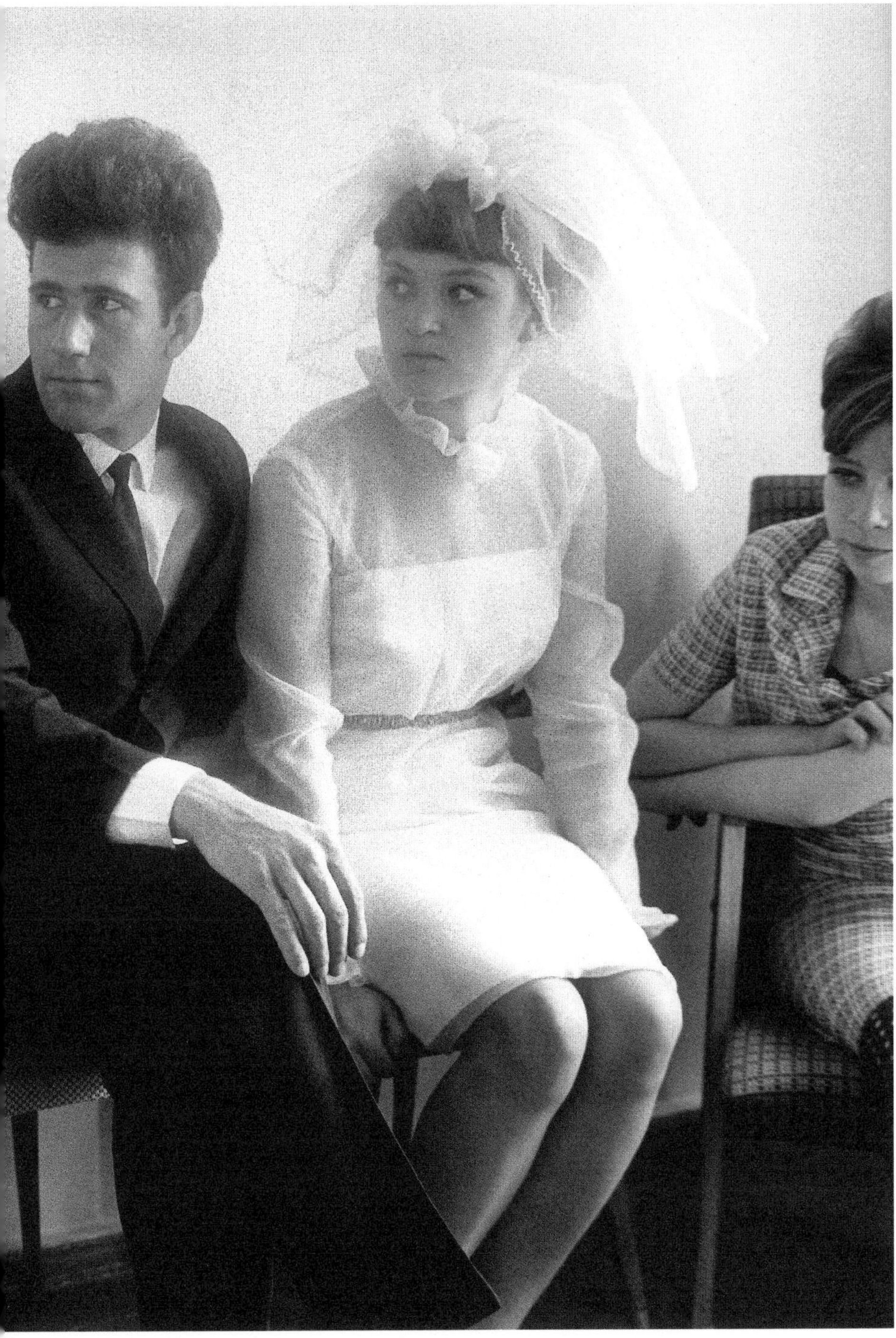

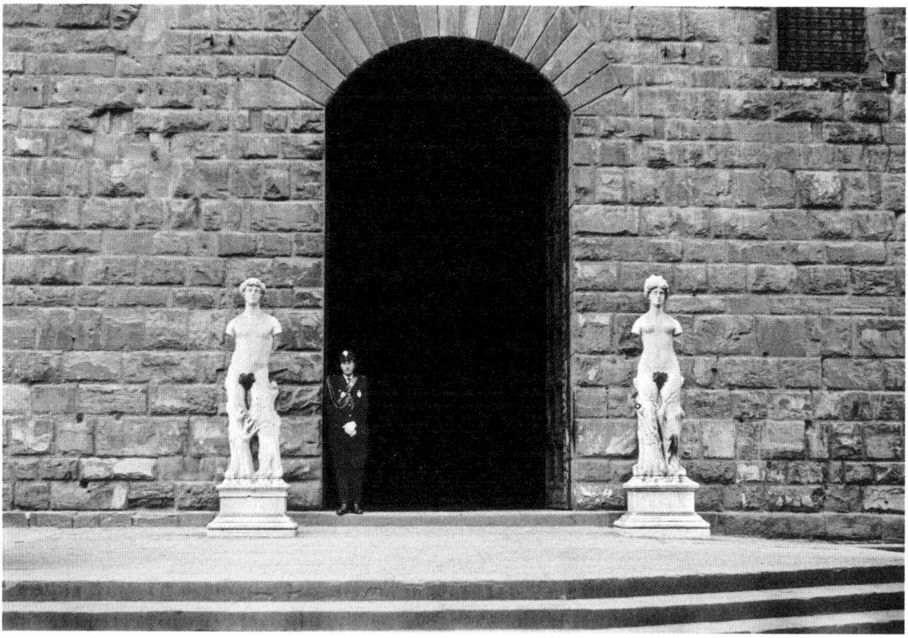

Florence, 1949

28 *Monday*

29 *Tuesday*

30 *Wednesday*

1 *Thursday*

2 *Friday*

3 *Saturday*

4 *Sunday*

5 Monday	Holiday (UK)
6 Tuesday	
7 Wednesday	
8 Thursday	
9 Friday	
10 Saturday	11 Sunday

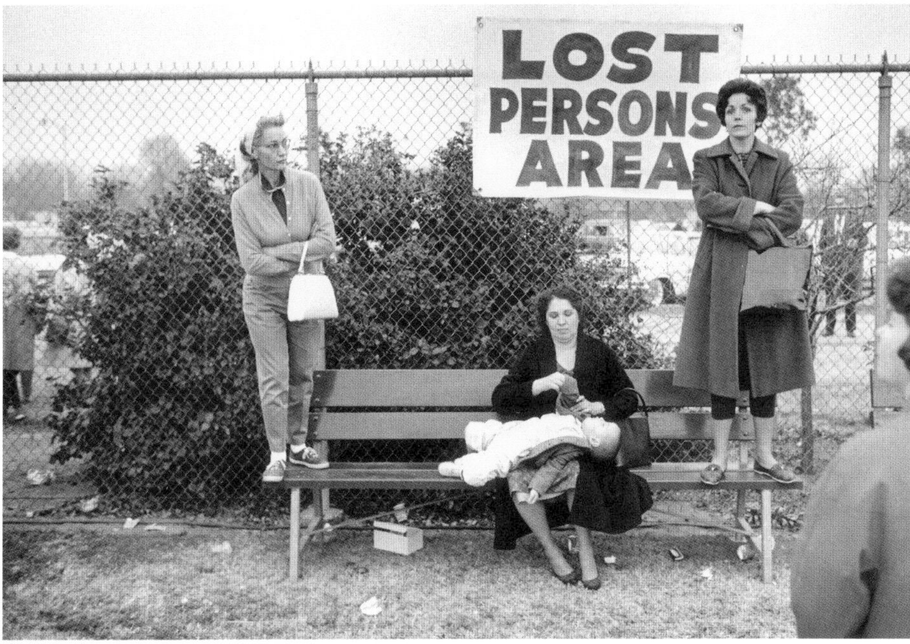

Pasadena, California, 1963

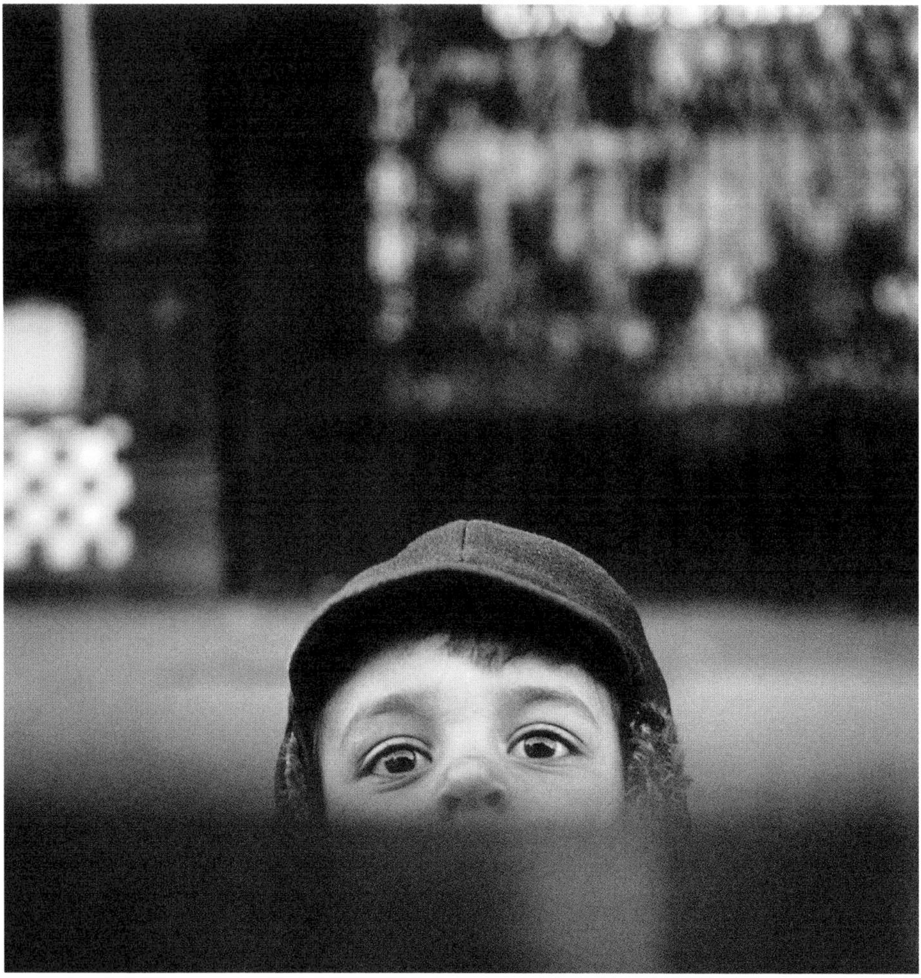

New York, 1951

12 *Monday*

13 *Tuesday*

14 *Wednesday*

15 *Thursday*

16 *Friday*

17 *Saturday*

18 *Sunday*

19 *Monday*

Holiday (Canada)

20 *Tuesday*

21 *Wednesday*

22 *Thursday*

23 *Friday*

24 *Saturday*

25 *Sunday*

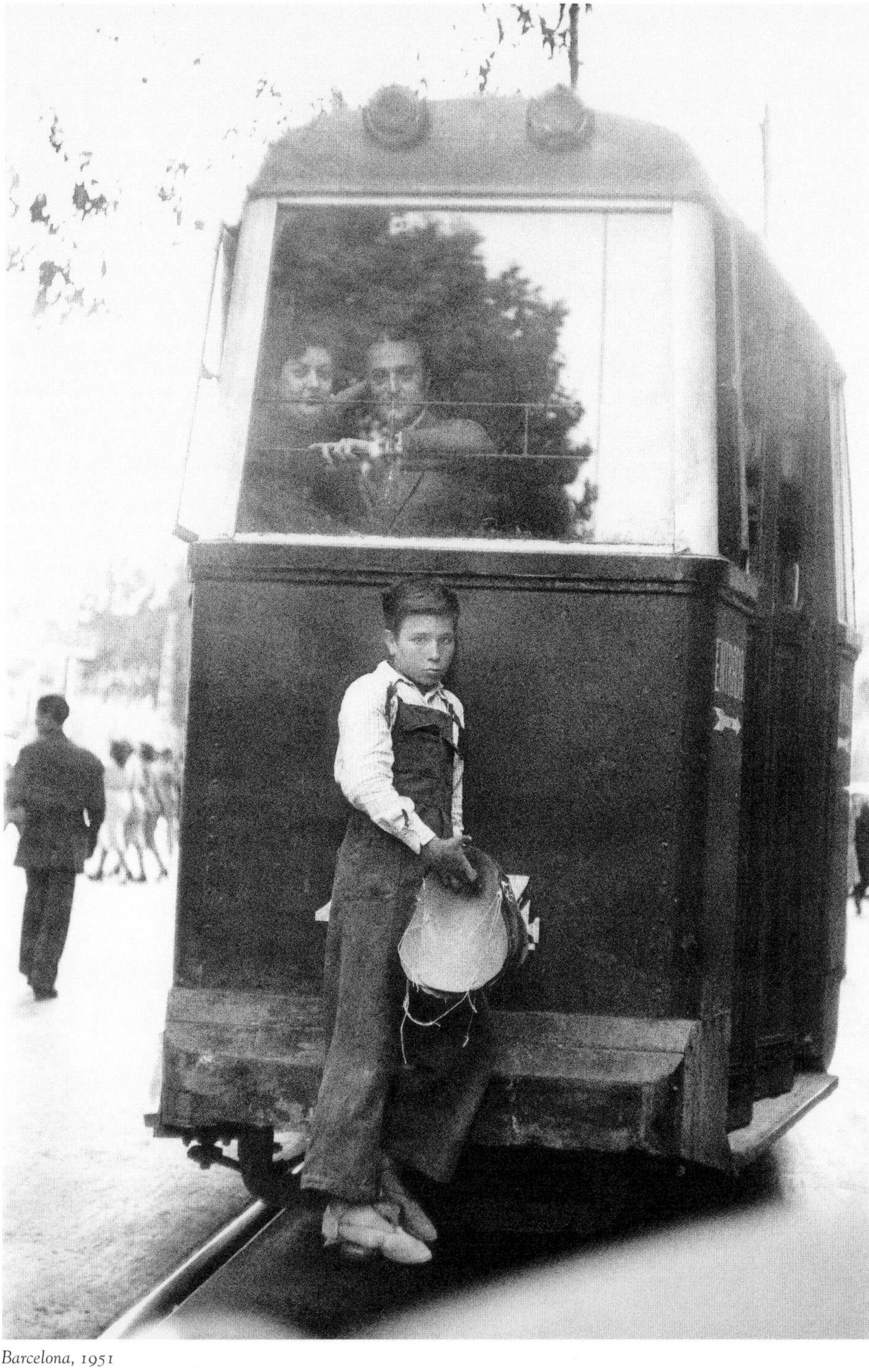

Barcelona, 1951

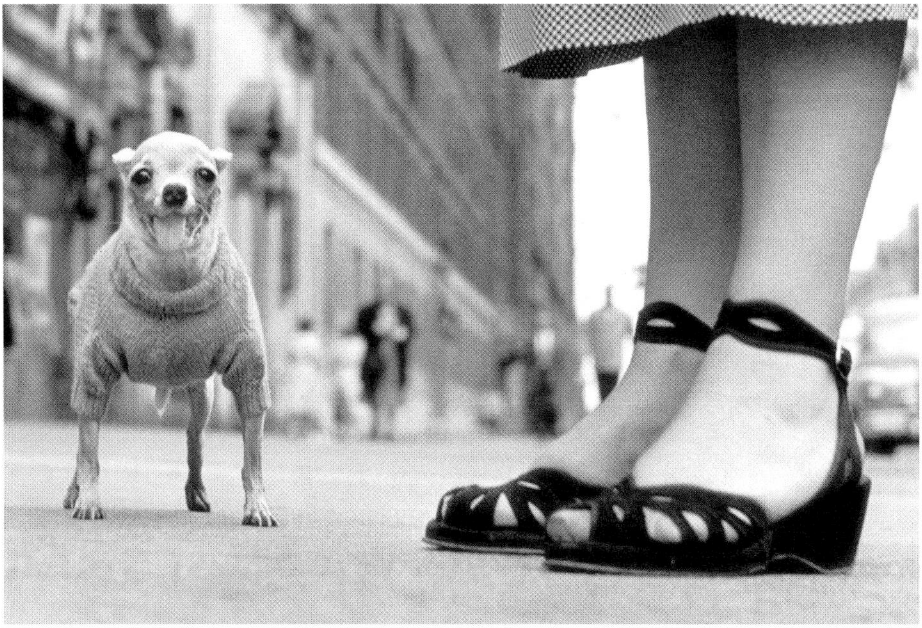

New York, 1946

26 *Monday*	Holiday (UK, USA)
27 *Tuesday*	
28 *Wednesday*	
29 *Thursday*	
30 *Friday*	
31 *Saturday*	1 *Sunday*

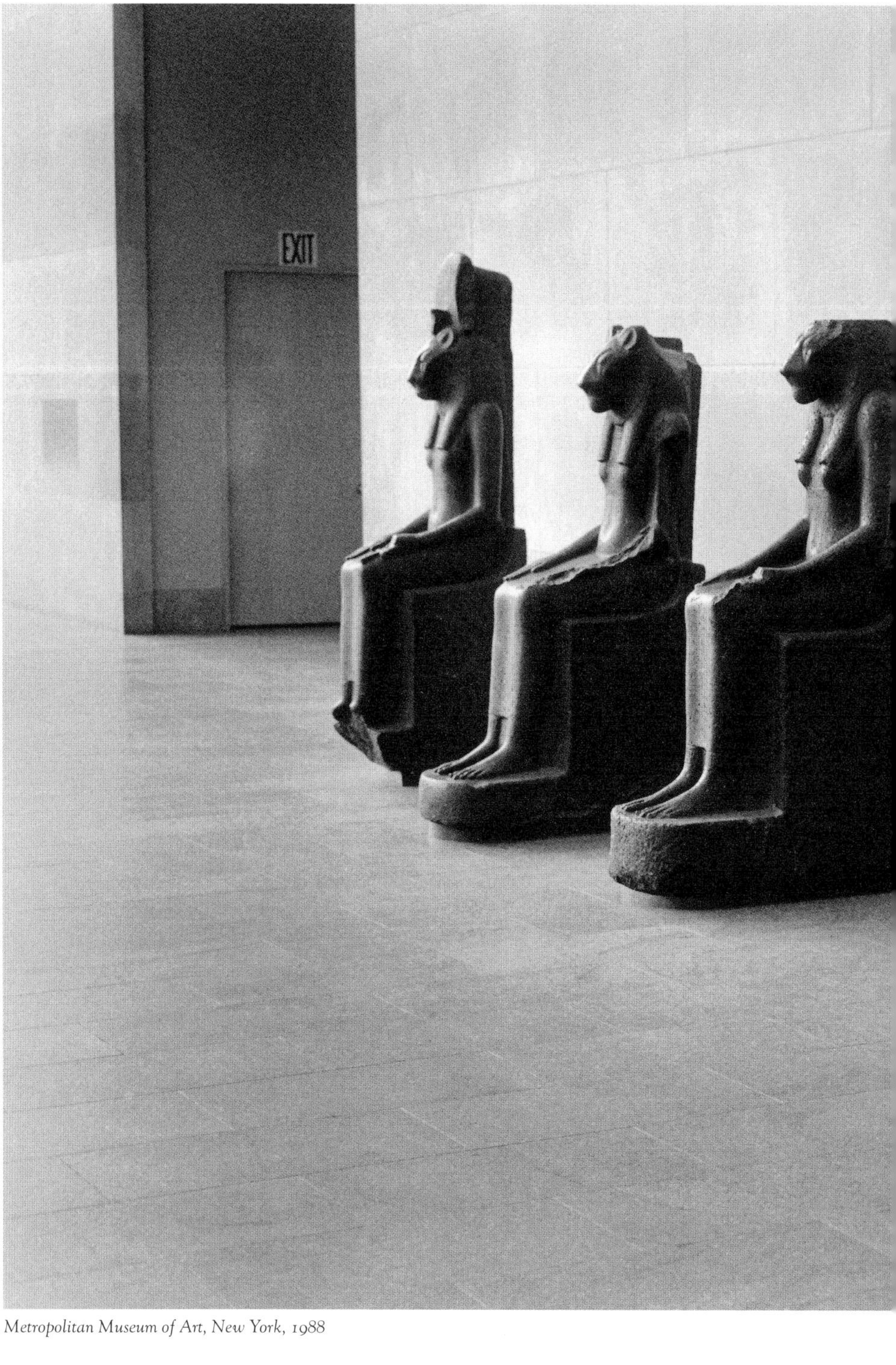

Metropolitan Museum of Art, New York, 1988

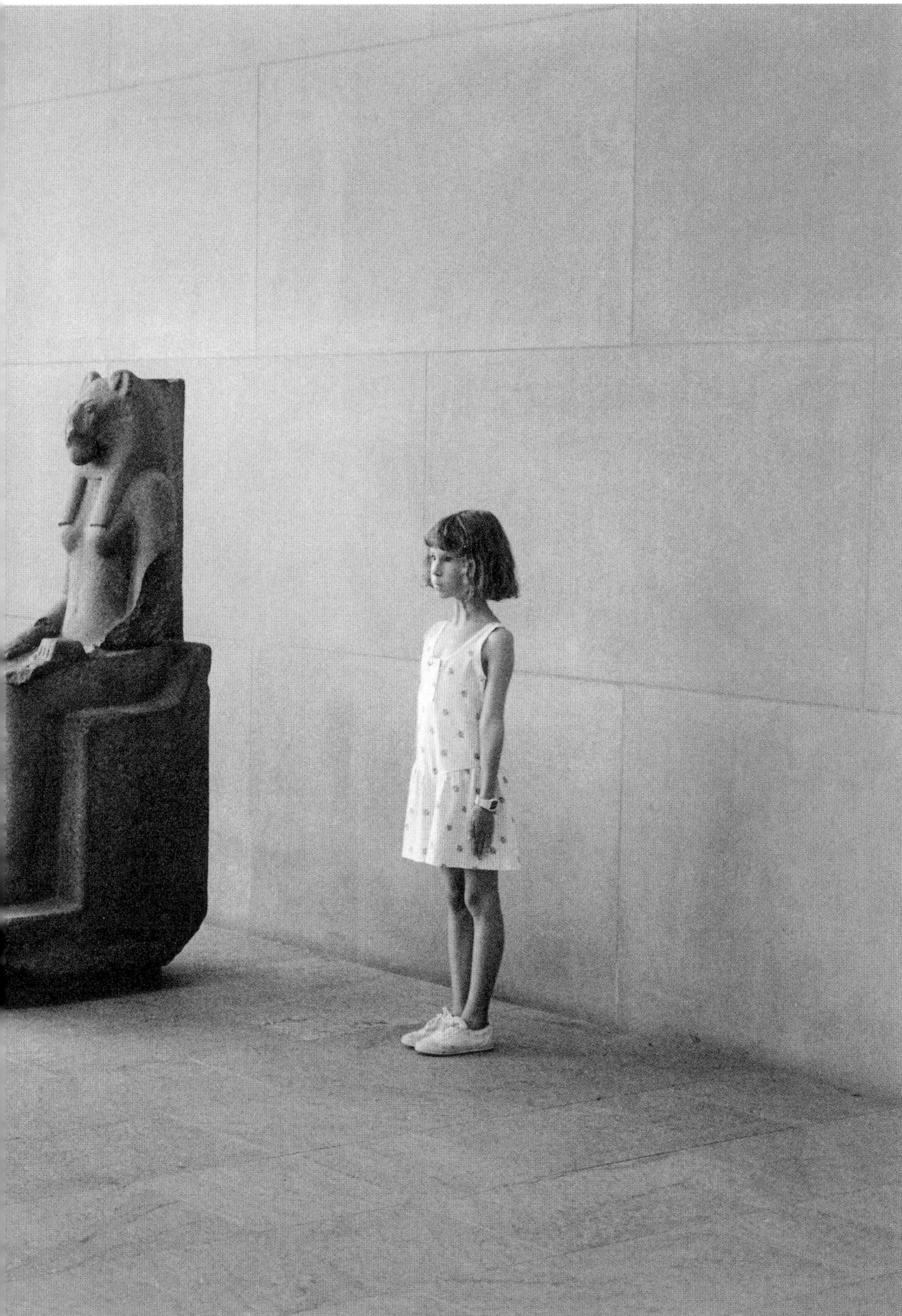

2 *Monday*

Holiday (New Zealand)

3 *Tuesday*

4 *Wednesday*

5 *Thursday*

6 *Friday*

7 *Saturday*

8 *Sunday*

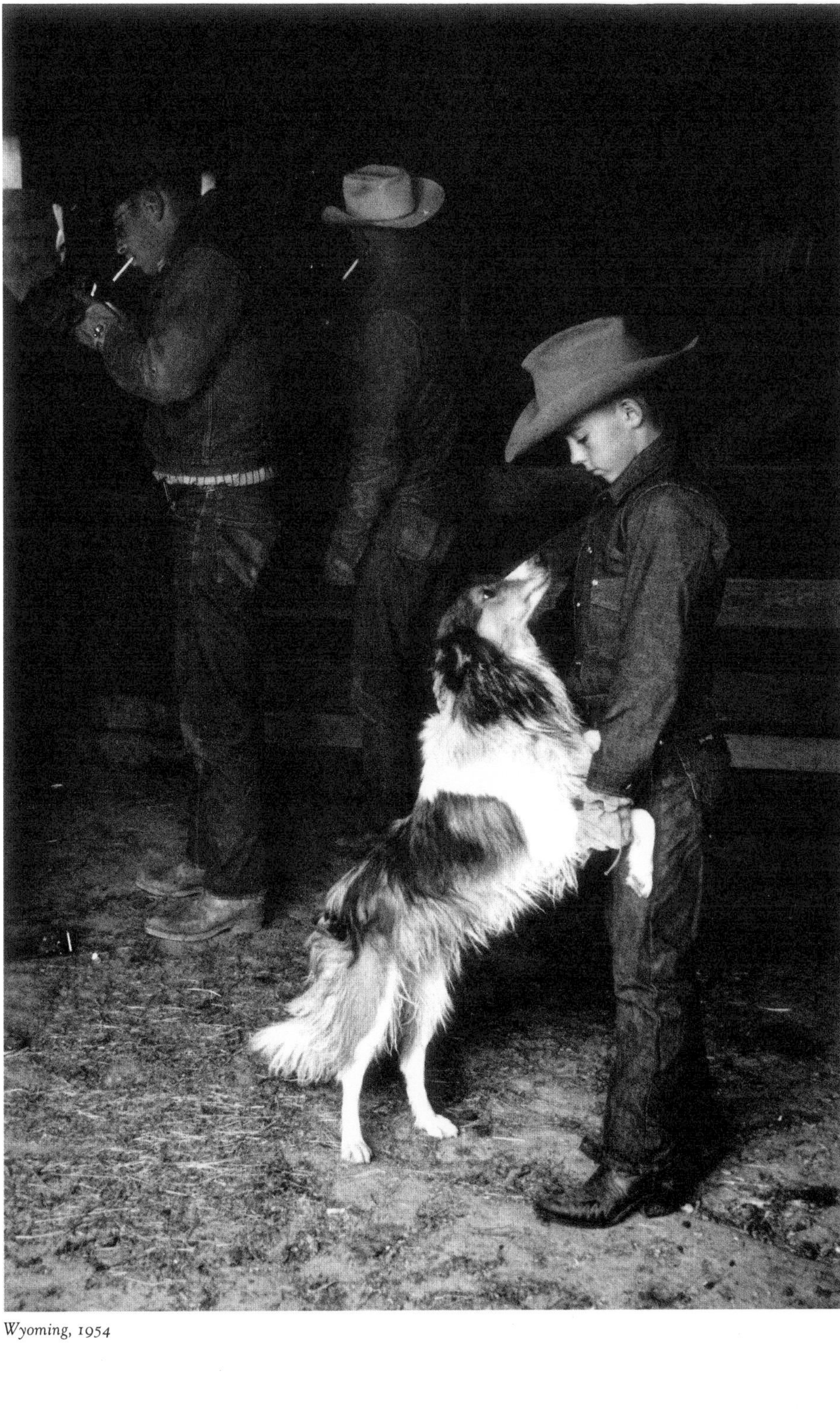

Wyoming, 1954

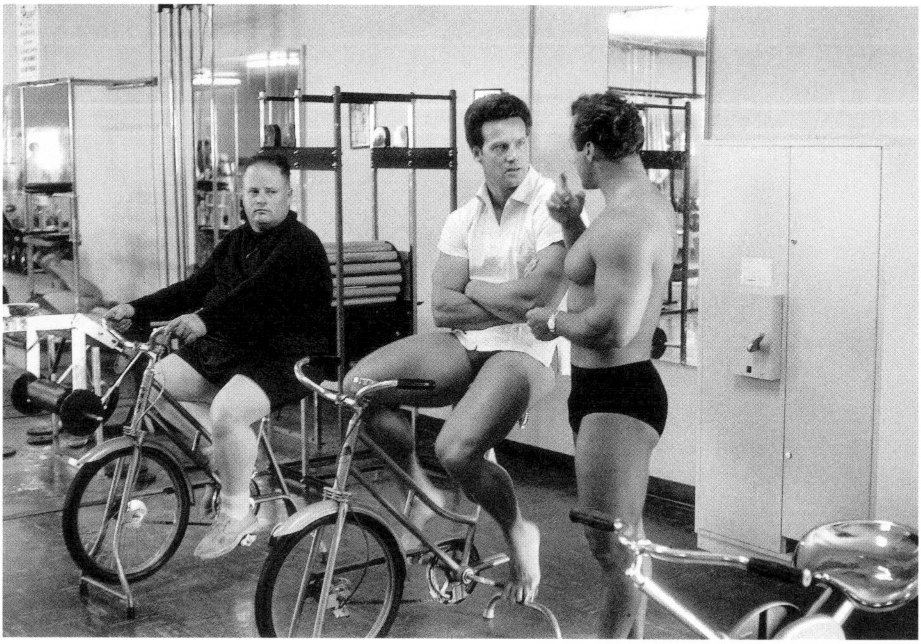

Los Angeles, 1957

9 *Monday*

10 *Tuesday*

11 *Wednesday*

12 *Thursday*

13 *Friday*

14 *Saturday*

15 *Sunday*

16 *Monday*

17 *Tuesday*

18 *Wednesday*

19 *Thursday*

20 *Friday*

21 *Saturday*

22 *Sunday*

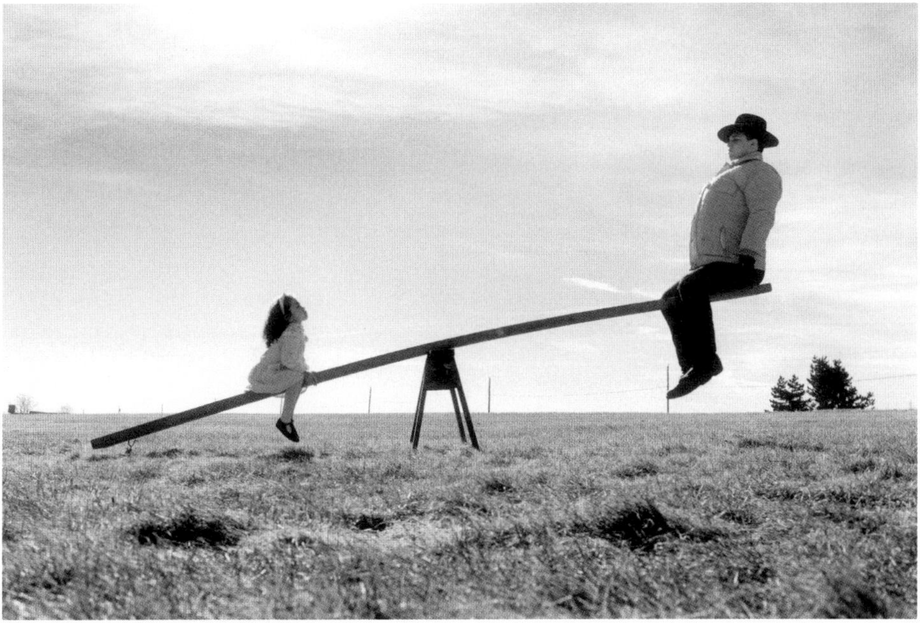

Bridgehampton, New York, 1990

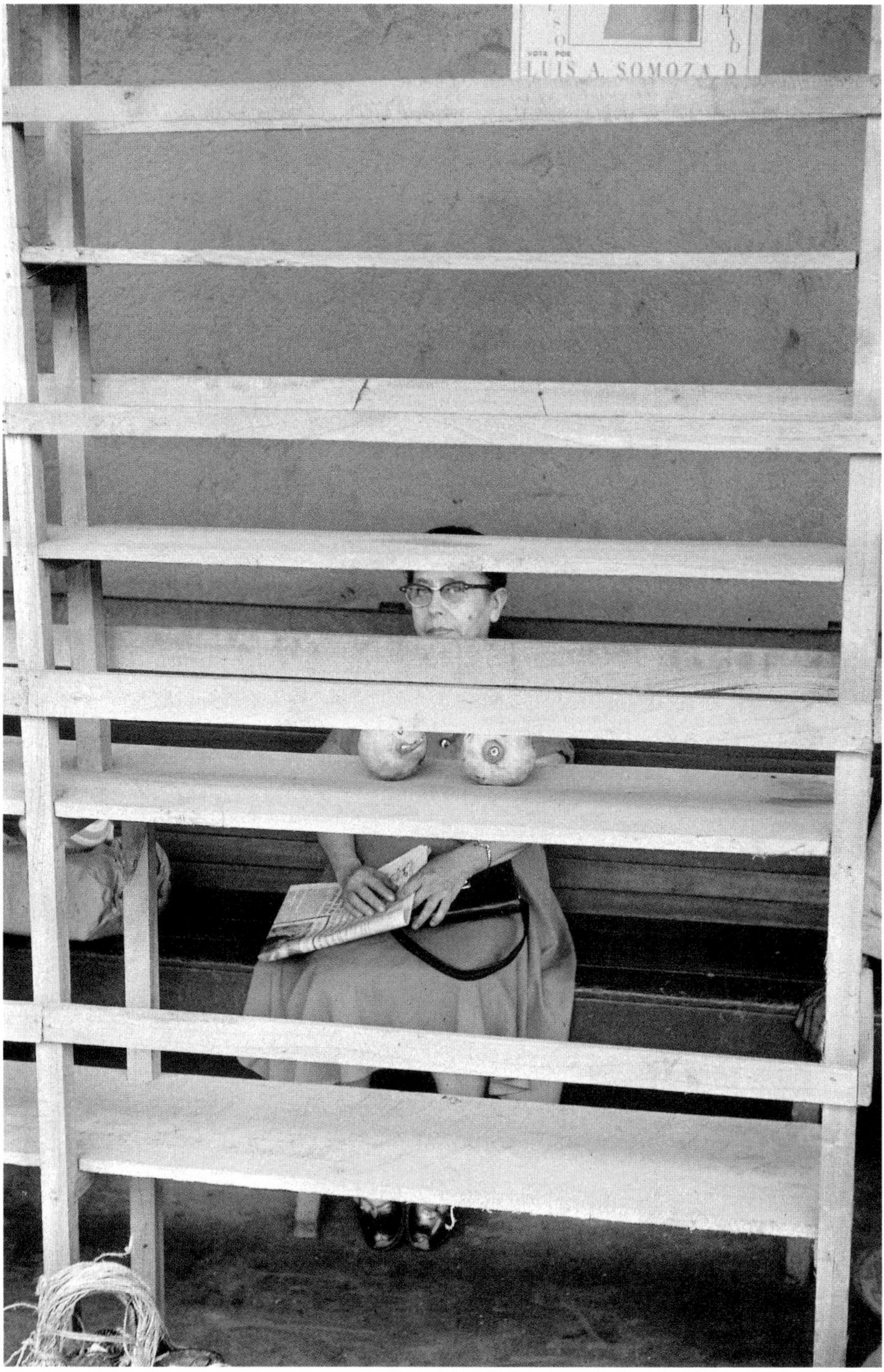

Managua, Nicaragua, 1957

23 *Monday*

24 *Tuesday*

25 *Wednesday*

26 *Thursday*

27 *Friday*

28 *Saturday*

29 *Sunday*

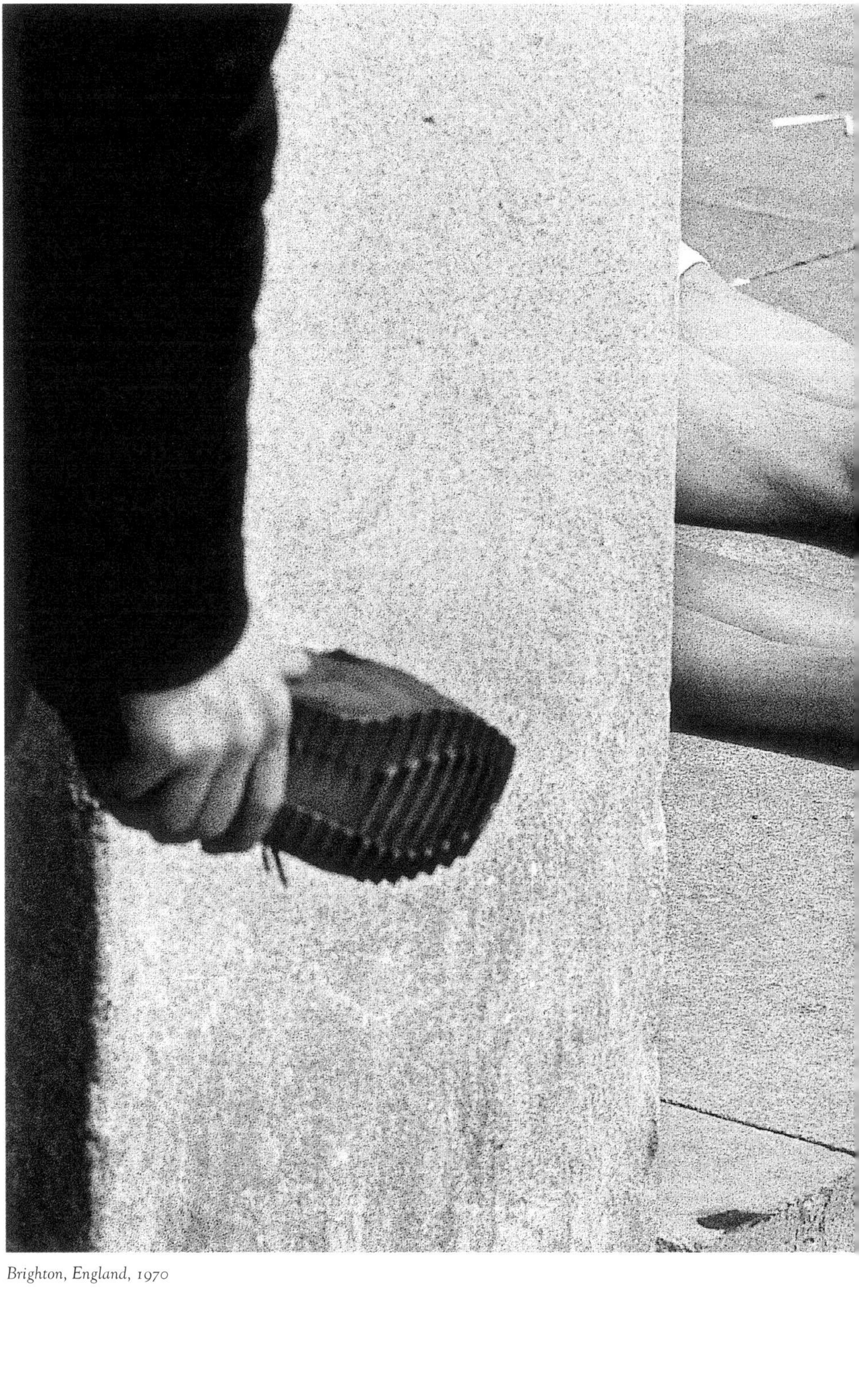

Brighton, England, 1970

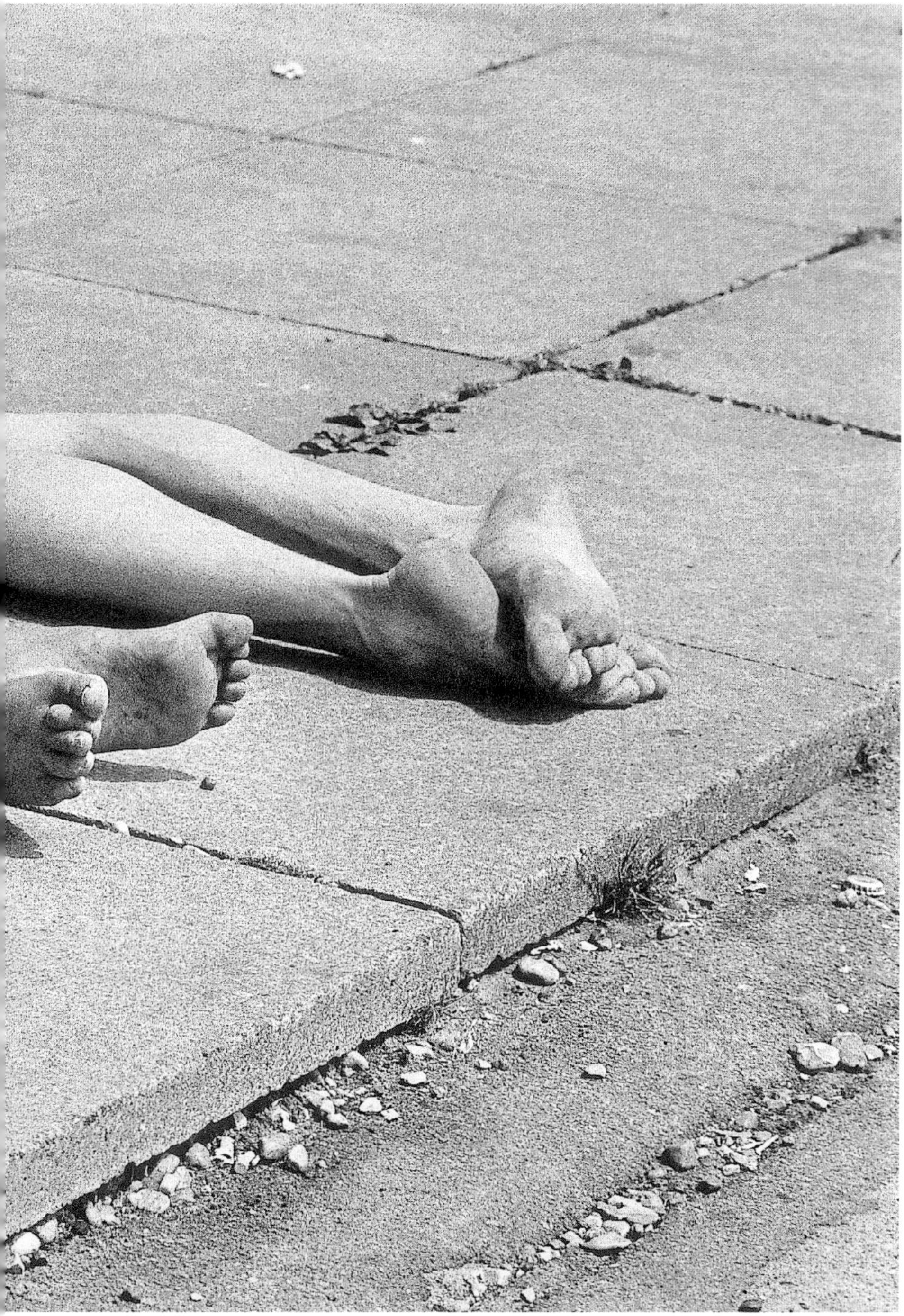

30 *Monday*

1 *Tuesday* Holiday (Canada)

2 *Wednesday*

3 *Thursday*

4 *Friday* Holiday (USA)

5 *Saturday*

6 *Sunday*

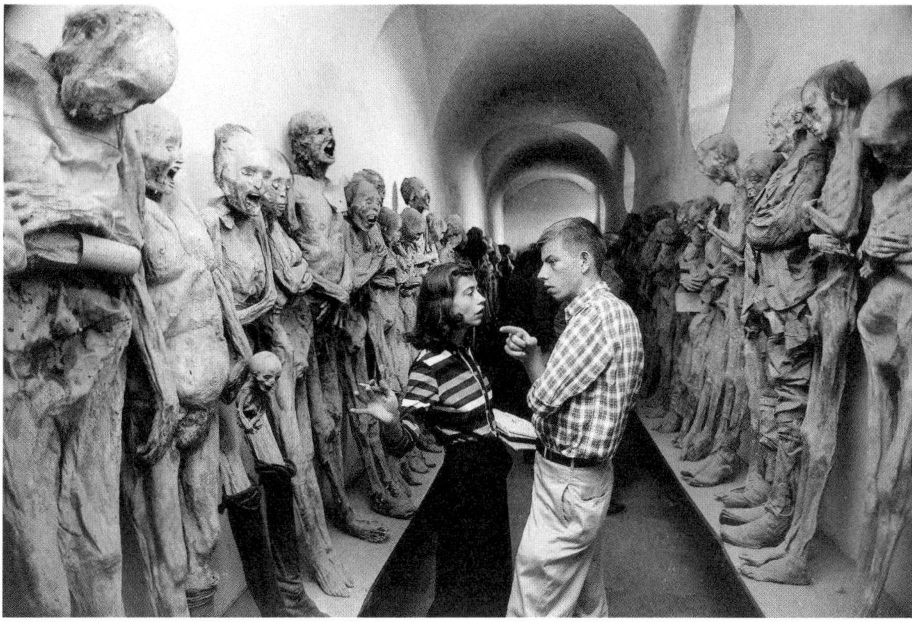

Guanajuato, Mexico, 1957

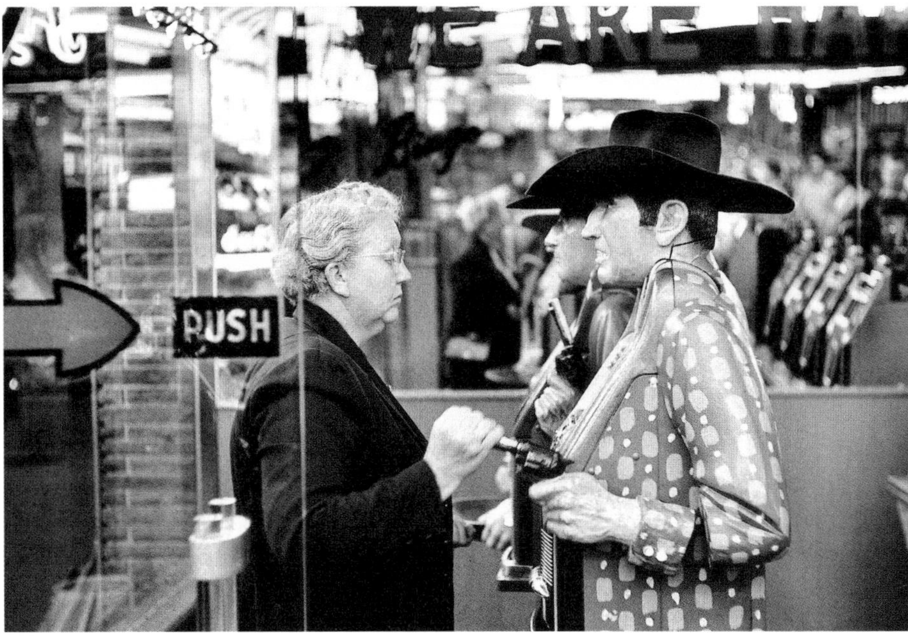

Las Vegas, 1954

7 Monday

8 Tuesday

9 Wednesday

10 Thursday

11 Friday

12 Saturday

13 Sunday

14 *Monday*

Holiday (N Ireland)

15 *Tuesday*

16 *Wednesday*

17 *Thursday*

18 *Friday*

19 *Saturday*

20 *Sunday*

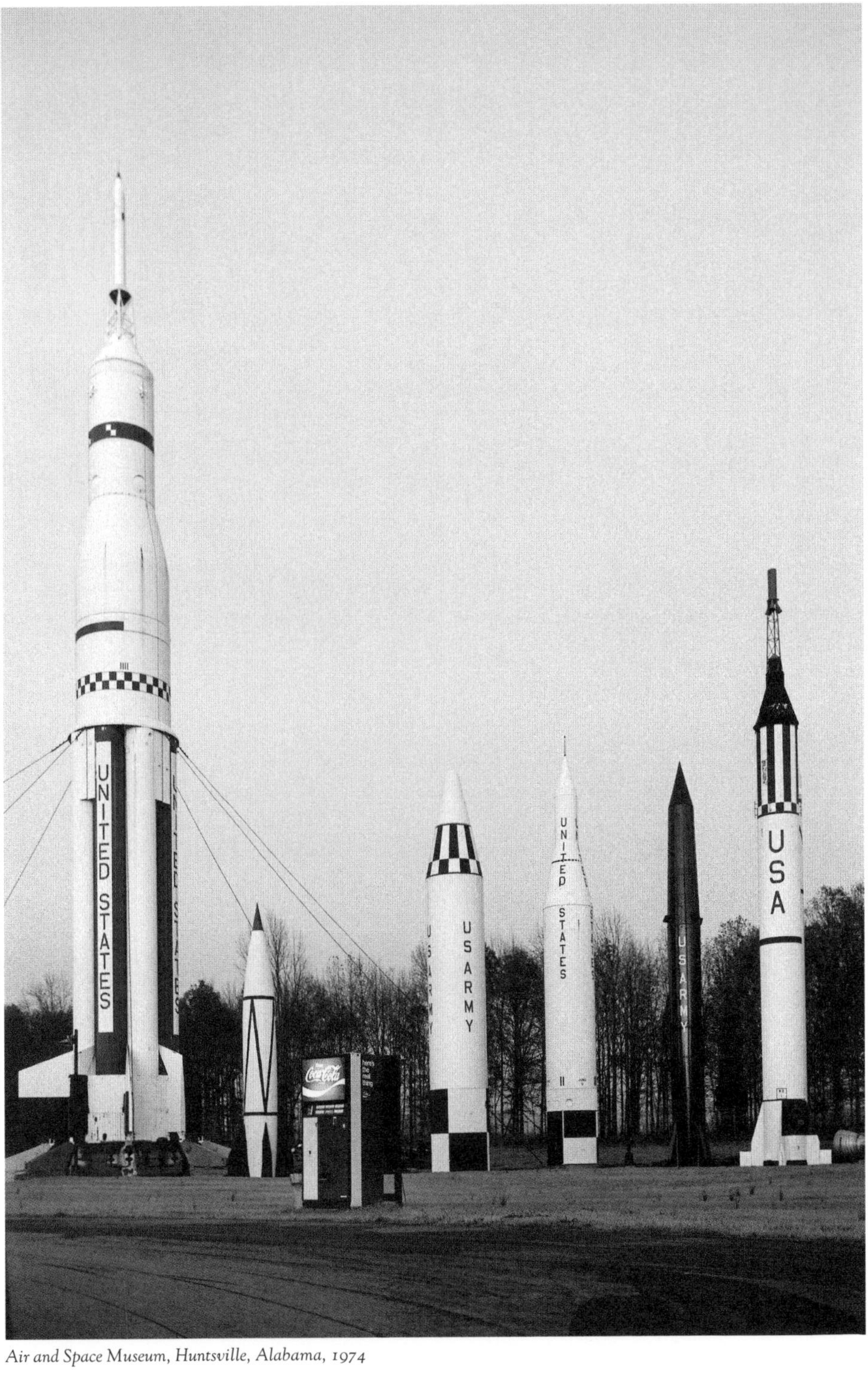

Air and Space Museum, Huntsville, Alabama, 1974

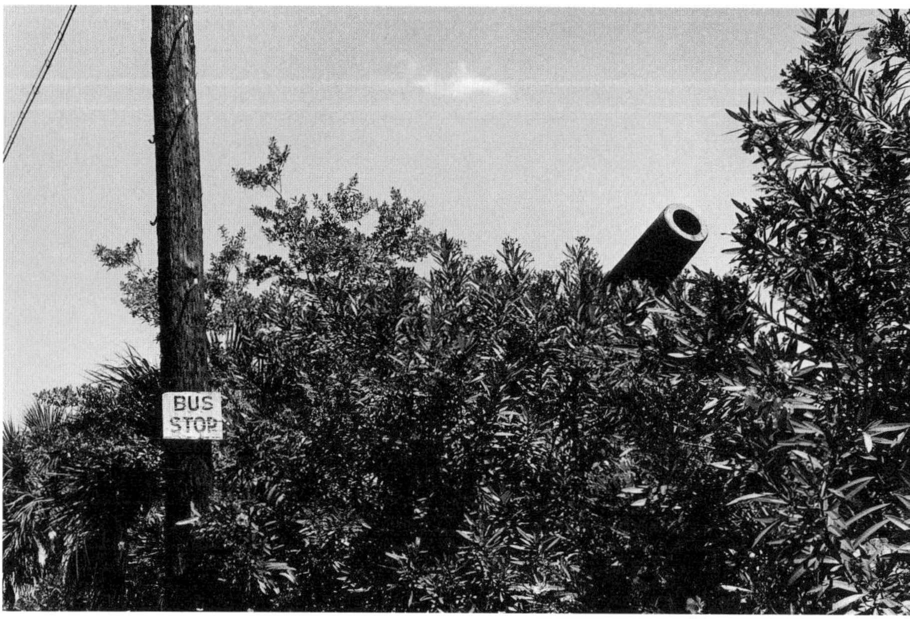

Fort Dix, New Jersey, 1951

21 Monday

22 Tuesday

23 Wednesday

24 Thursday

25 Friday

26 Saturday

27 Sunday

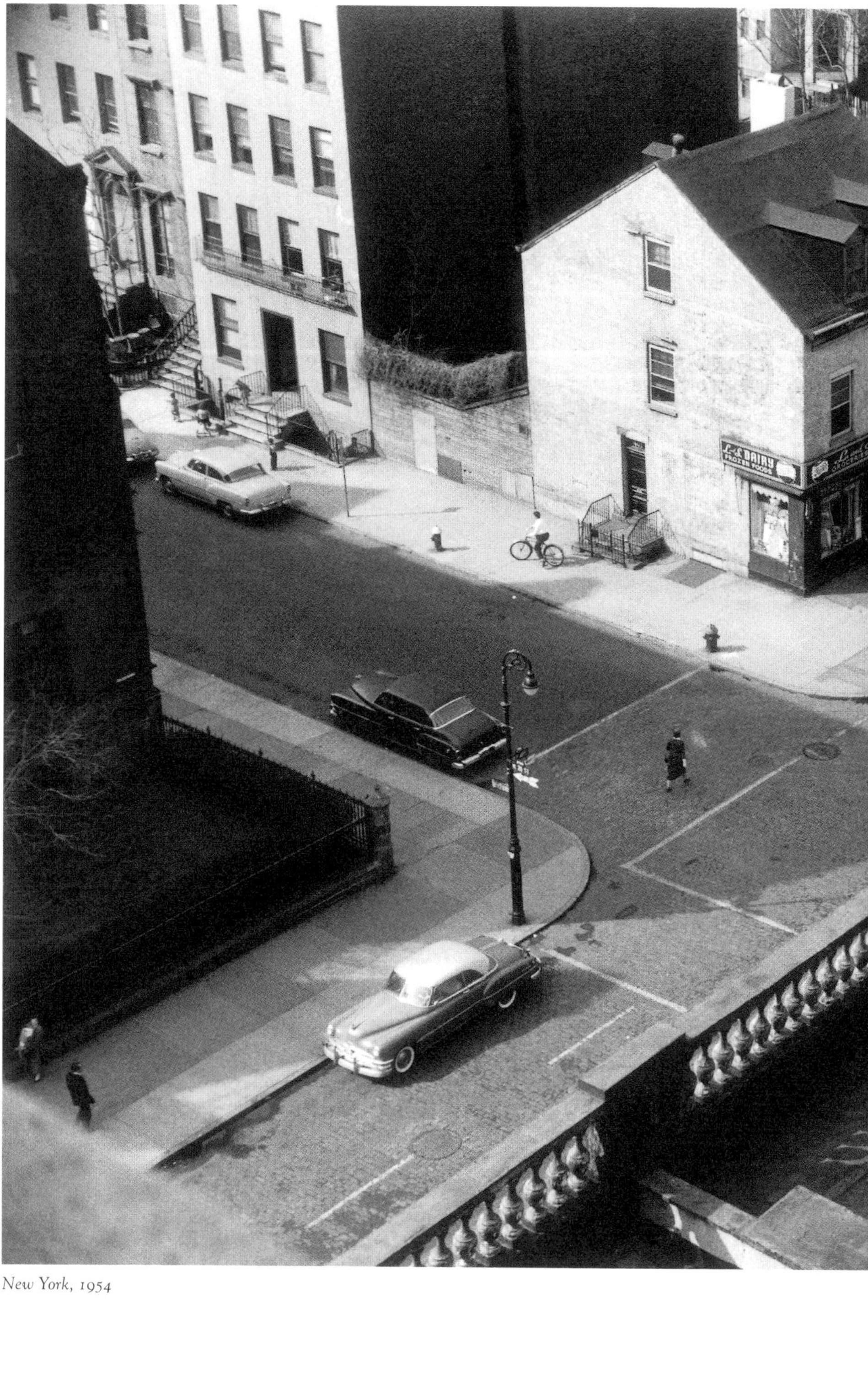

New York, 1954

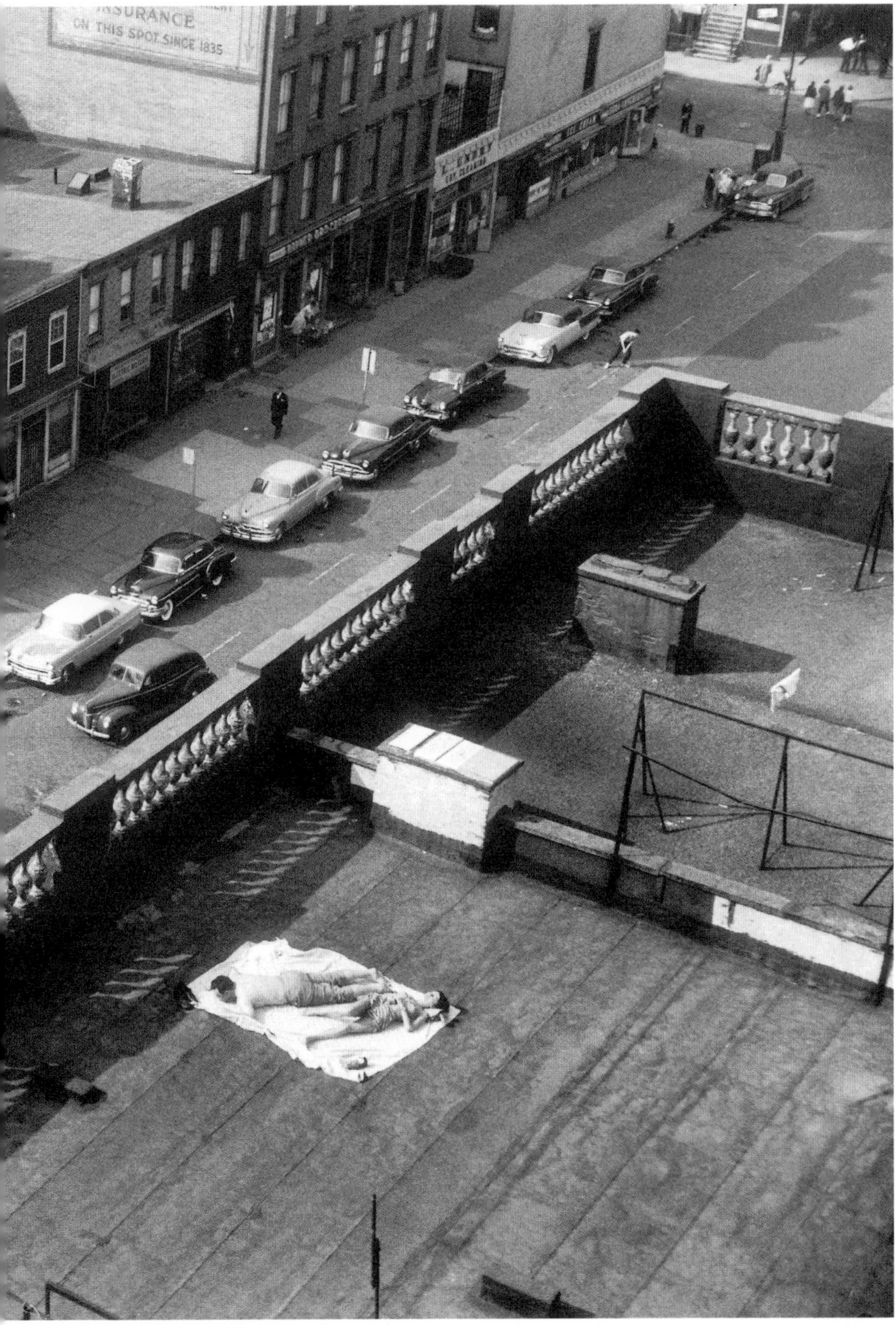
INSURANCE
ON THIS SPOT SINCE 1835

28 Monday

29 Tuesday

30 Wednesday

31 Thursday

1 Friday

2 Saturday

3 Sunday

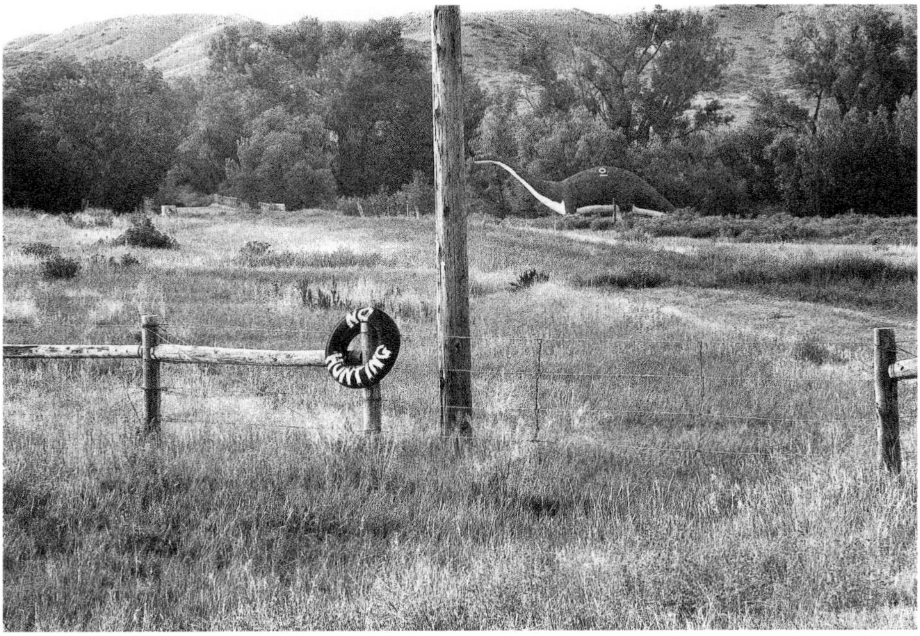

North Dakota, 1969

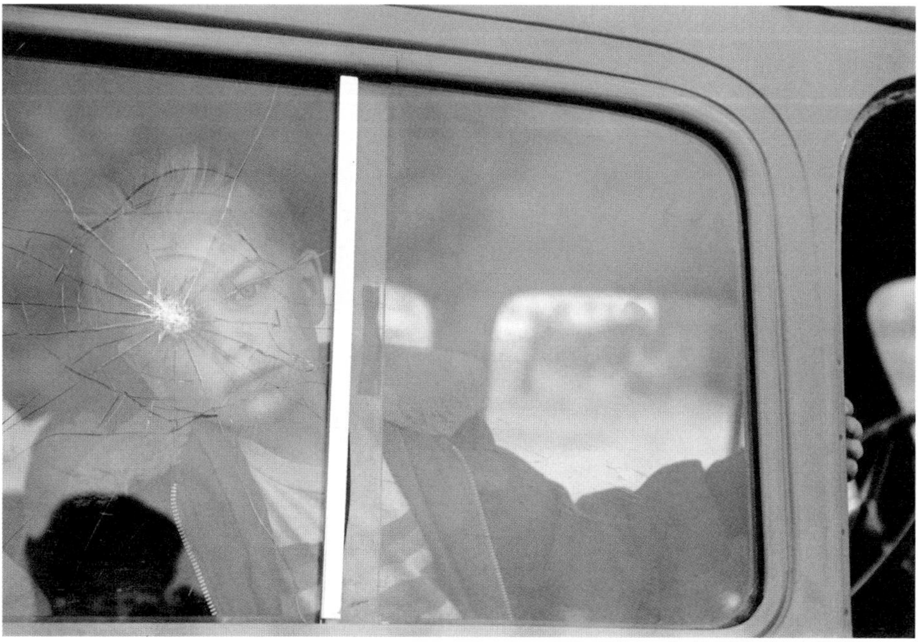

Colorado, 1955

4 *Monday* Holiday (Scotland)

5 *Tuesday*

6 *Wednesday*

7 *Thursday*

8 *Friday*

9 *Saturday*

10 *Sunday*

11 Monday

12 Tuesday

13 Wednesday

14 Thursday

15 Friday

16 Saturday

17 Sunday

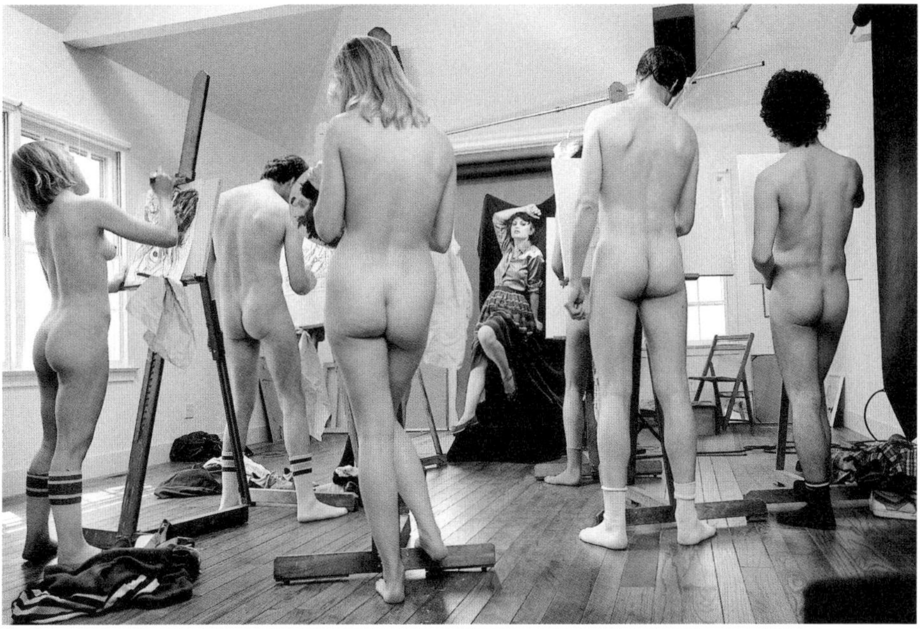

East Hampton, New York, 1983

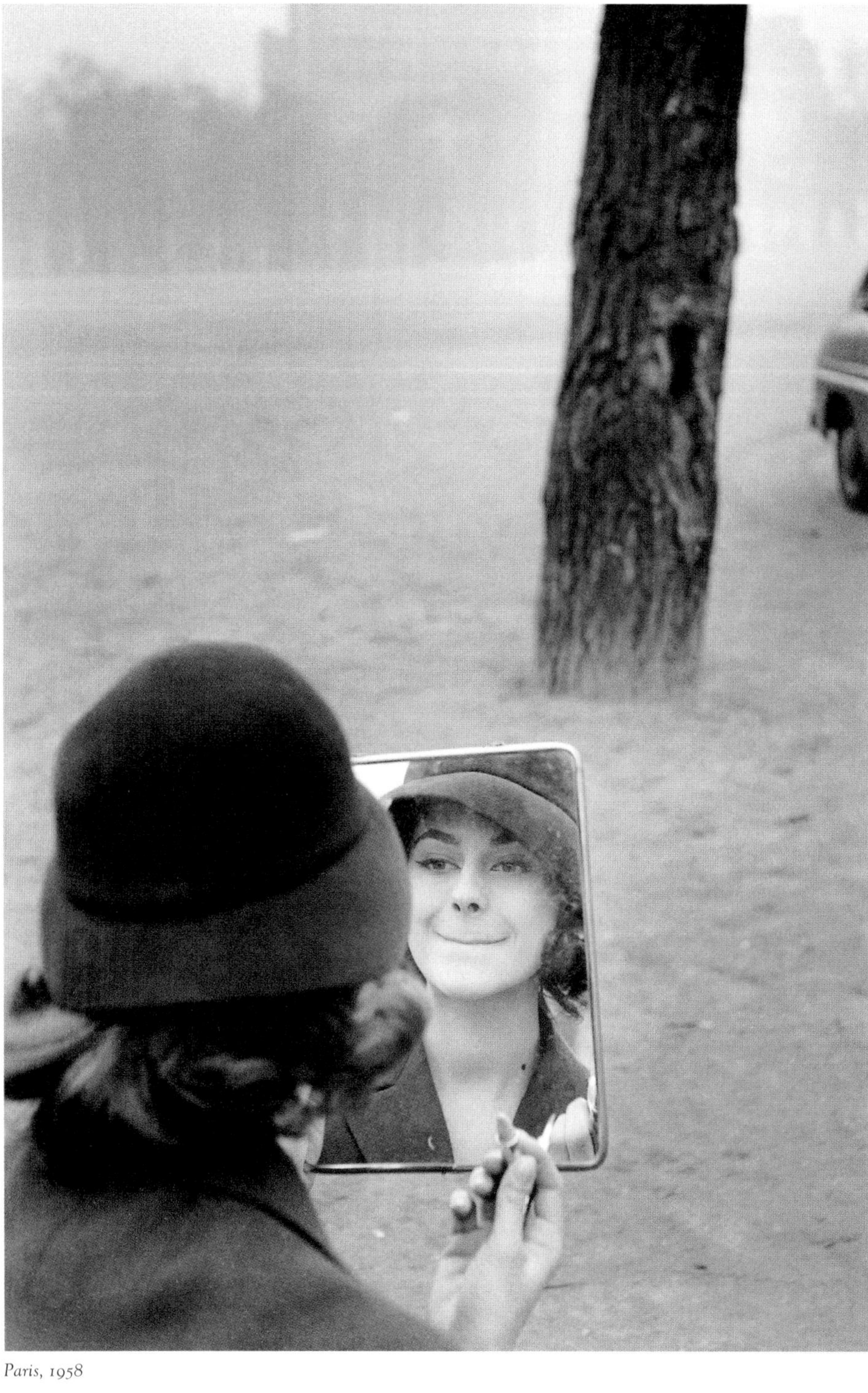

Paris, 1958

18 *Monday*

19 *Tuesday*

20 *Wednesday*

21 *Thursday*

22 *Friday*

23 *Saturday*

24 *Sunday*

25 Monday

Holiday
(UK except Scotland)

26 Tuesday

27 Wednesday

28 Thursday

29 Friday

30 Saturday

31 Sunday

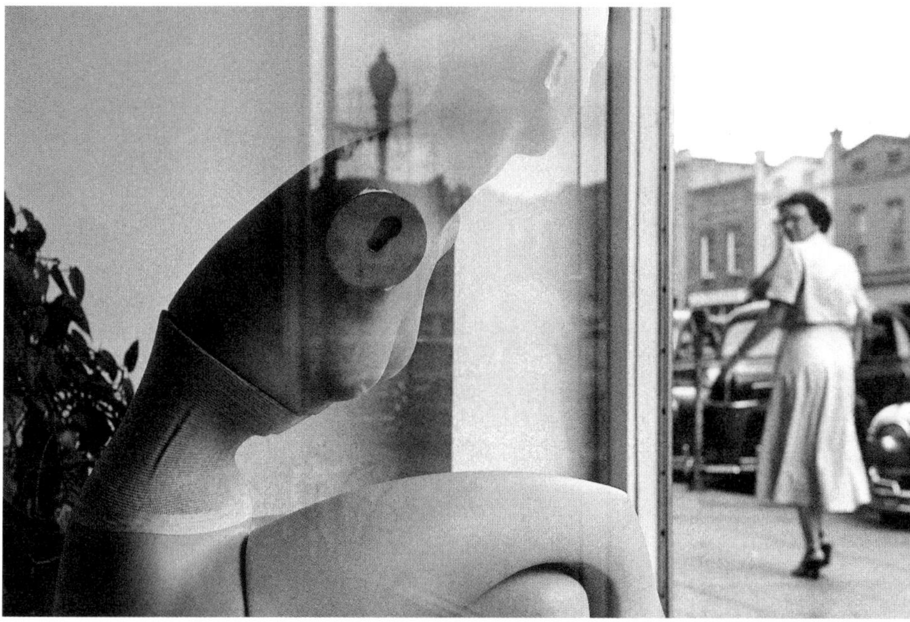

Wilmington, North Carolina, 1950

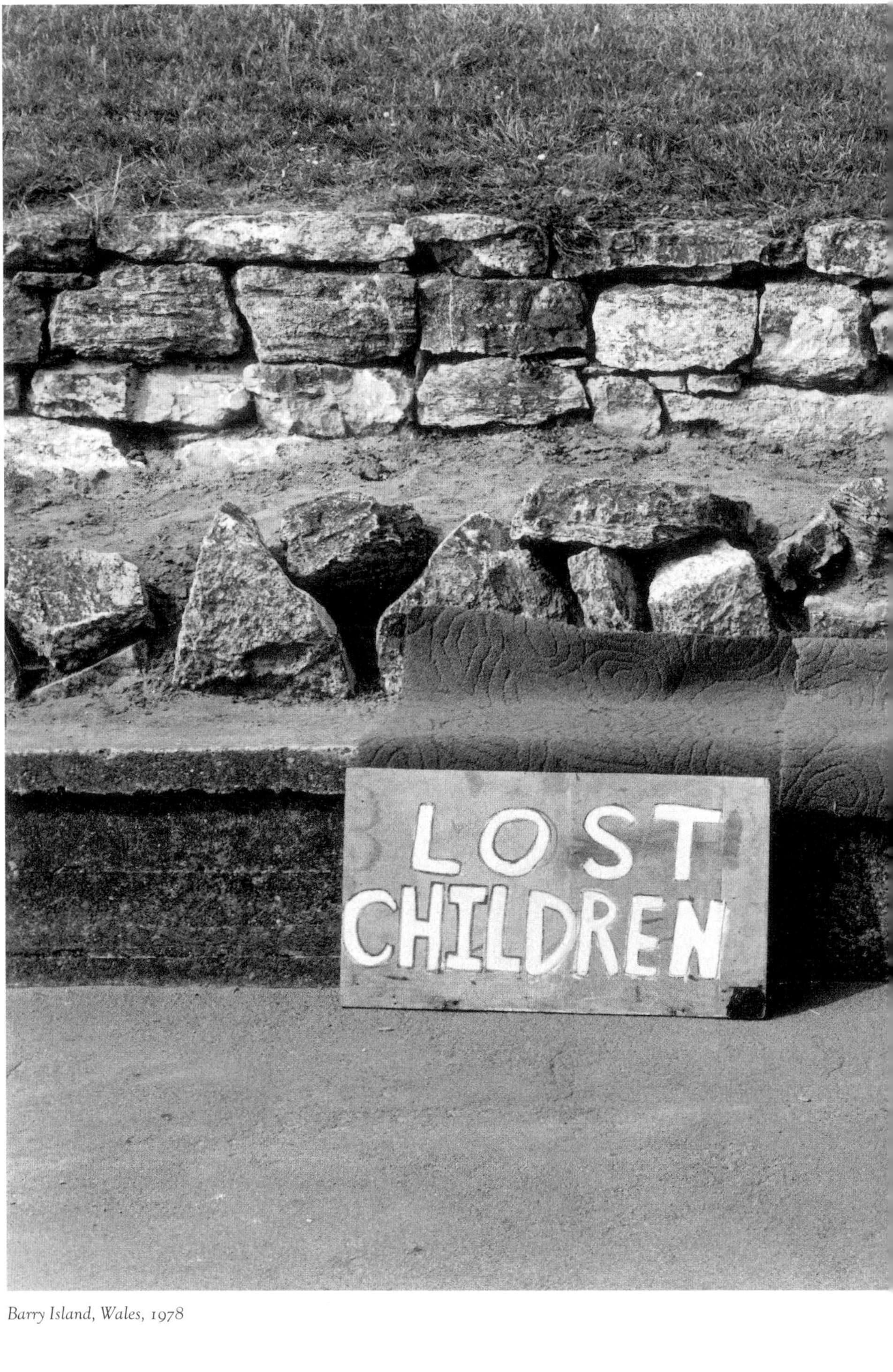

Barry Island, Wales, 1978

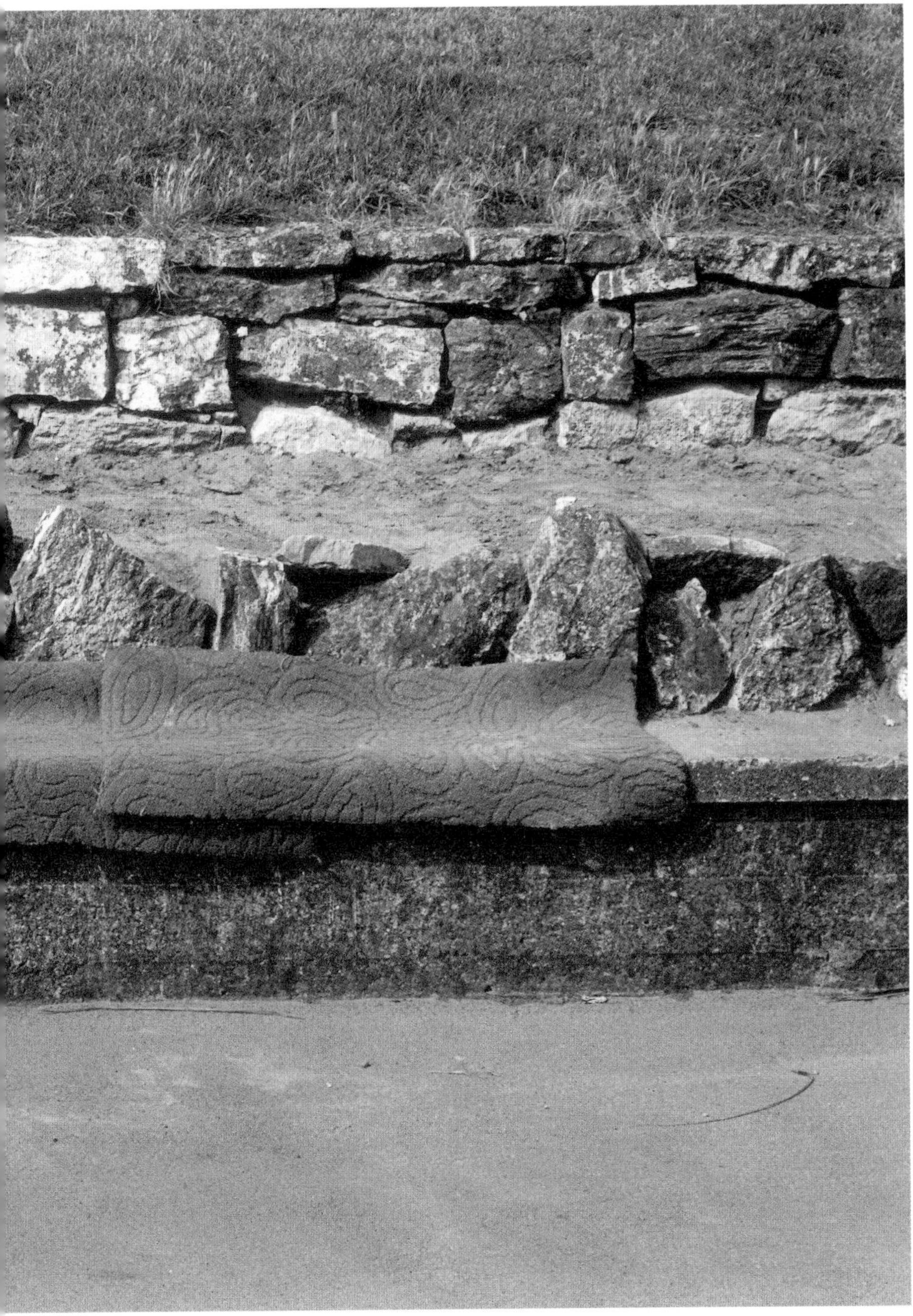

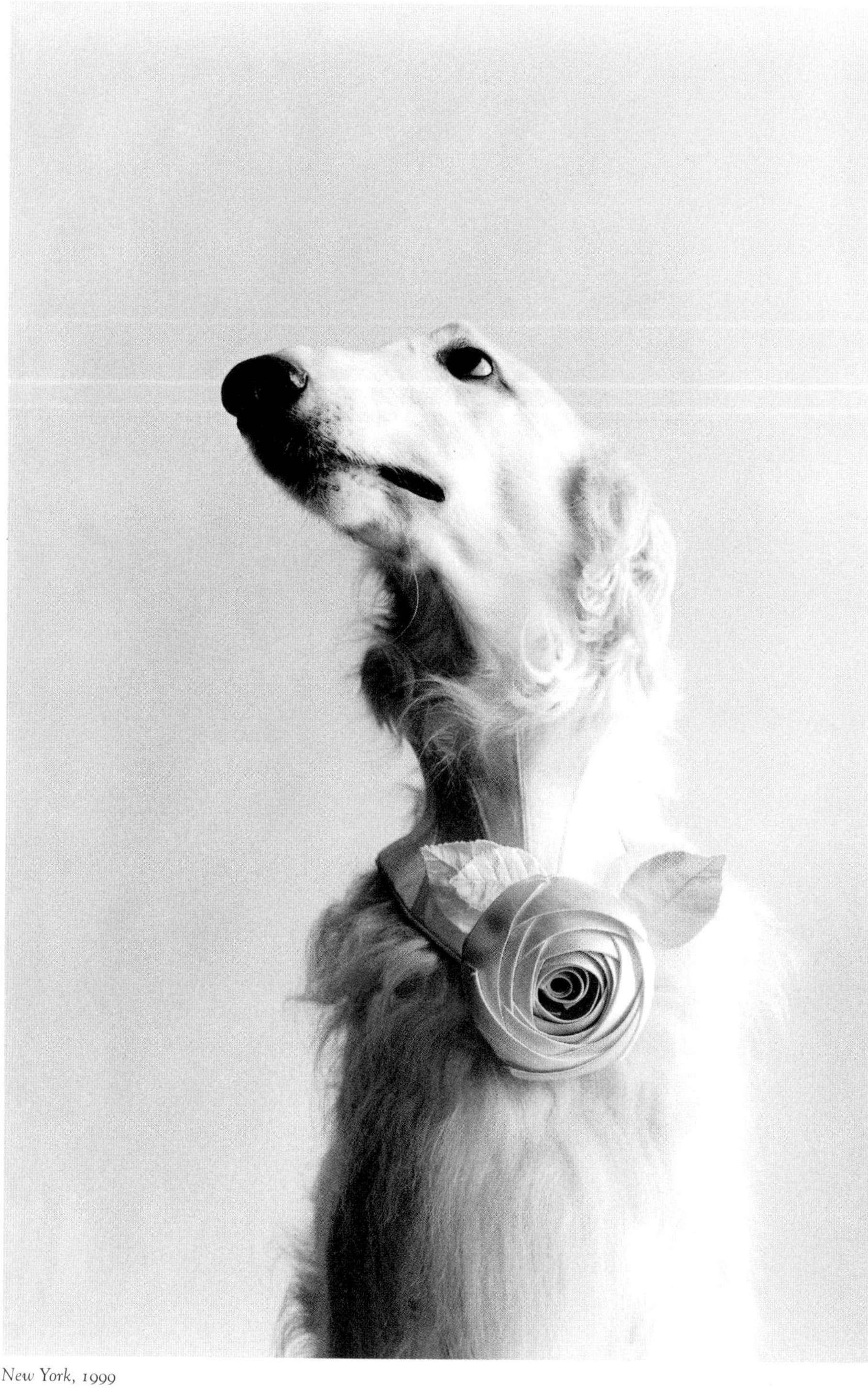

New York, 1999

1 Monday	Holiday (Canada, USA)
2 Tuesday	
3 Wednesday	
4 Thursday	
5 Friday	
6 Saturday	7 Sunday

8 *Monday*	
9 *Tuesday*	
10 *Wednesday*	
11 *Thursday*	
12 *Friday*	
13 *Saturday*	14 *Sunday*

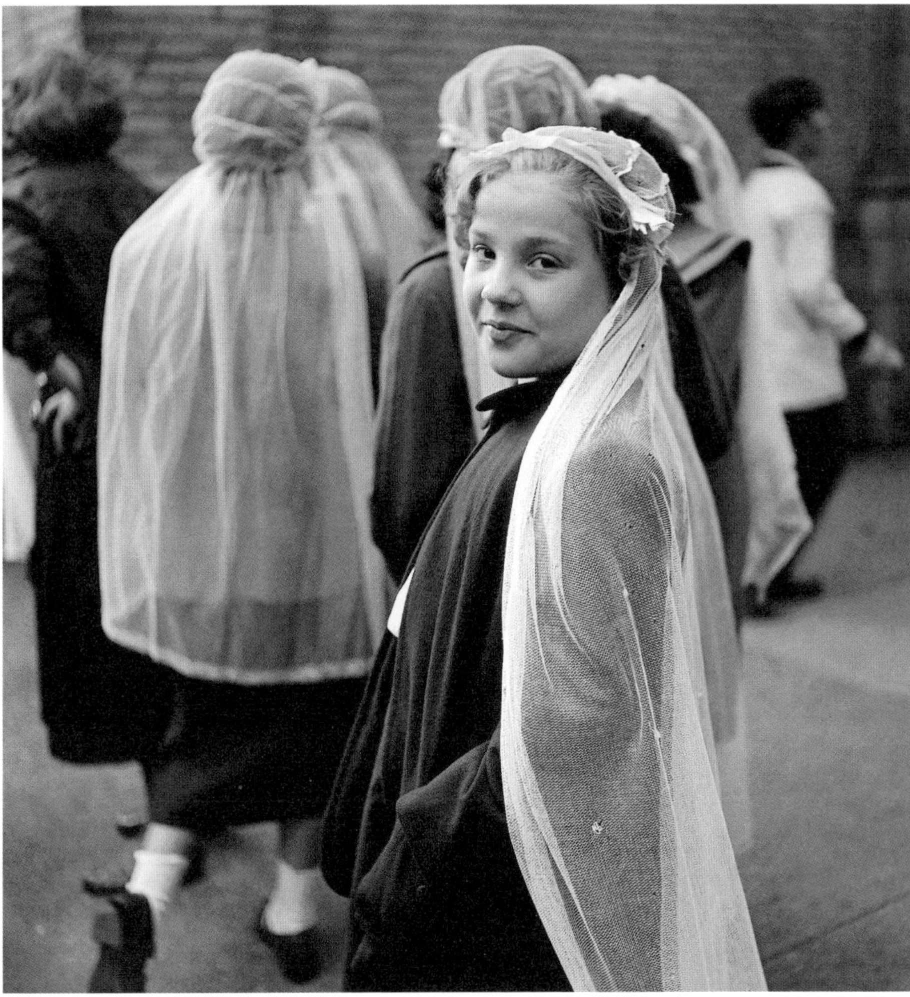

New York, 1949

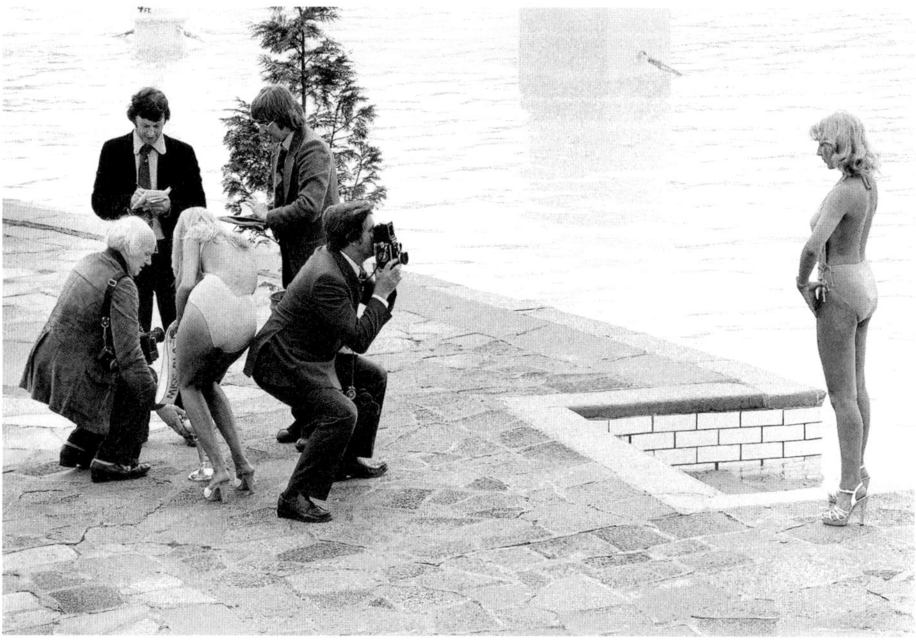

Blackpool, England, 1978

15 *Monday*

16 *Tuesday*

17 *Wednesday*

18 *Thursday*

19 *Friday*

20 *Saturday*

21 *Sunday*

22 *Monday*

23 *Tuesday*

24 *Wednesday*

25 *Thursday*

26 *Friday*

27 *Saturday*

28 *Sunday*

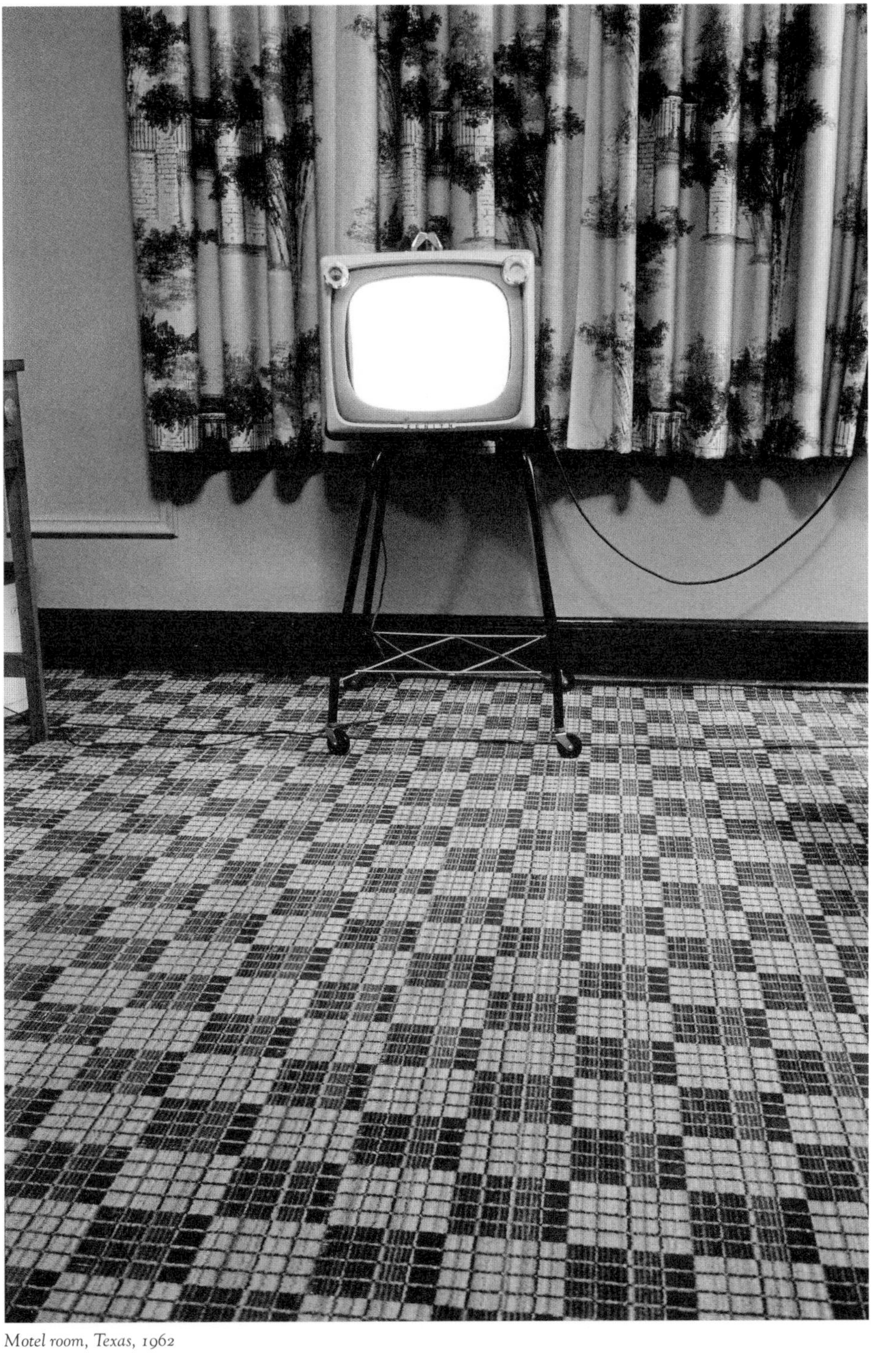

Motel room, Texas, 1962

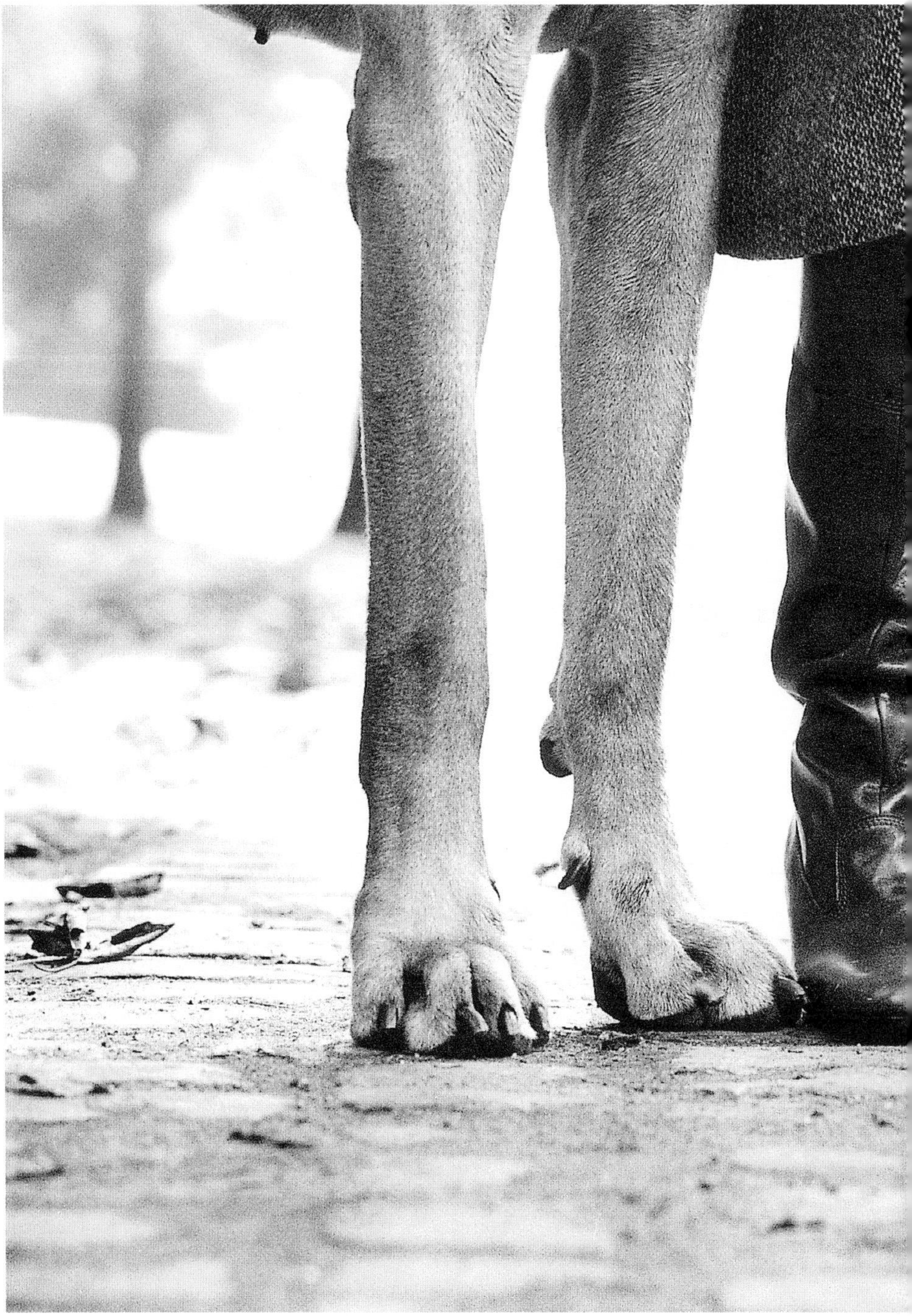

New York, 1974

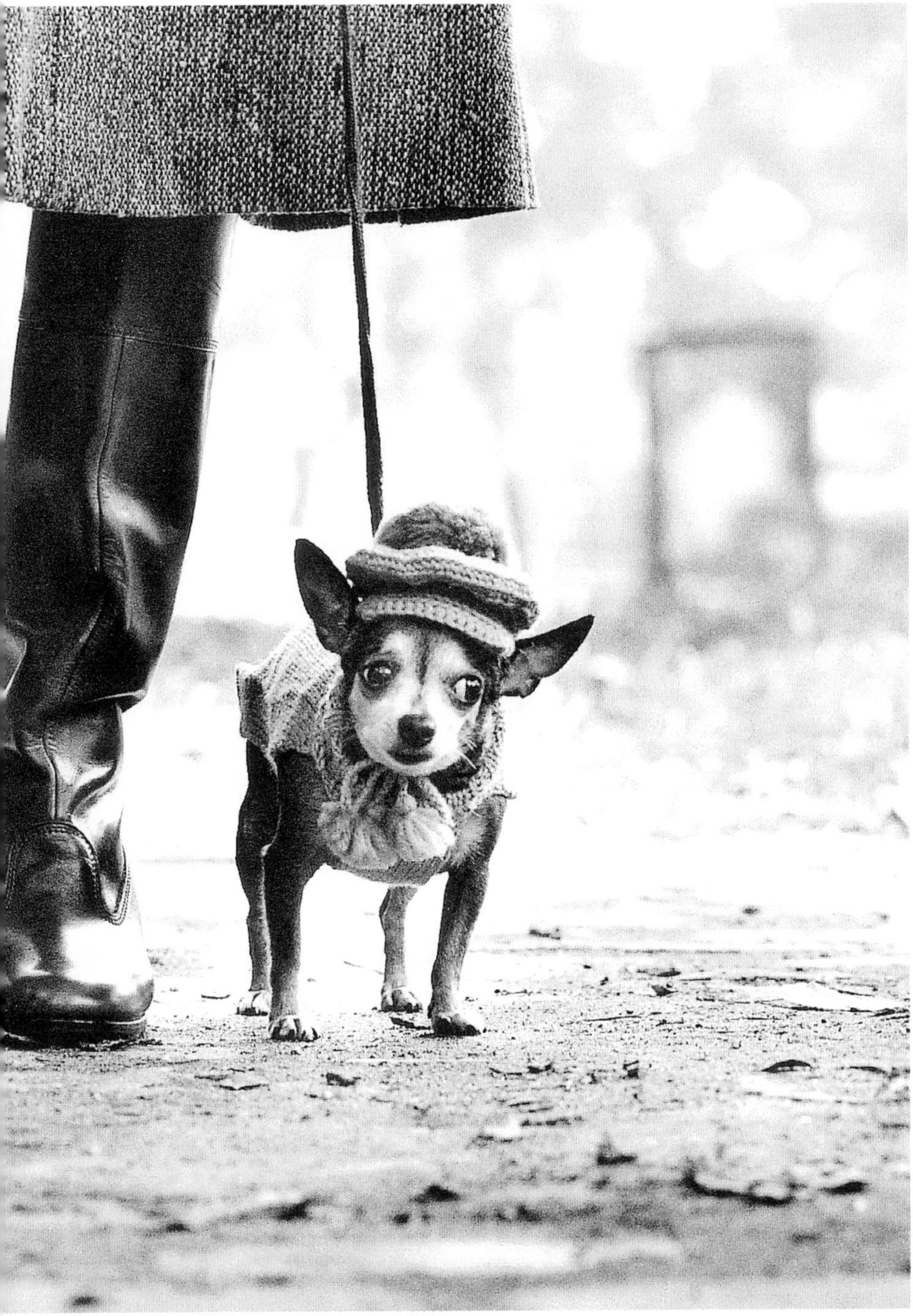

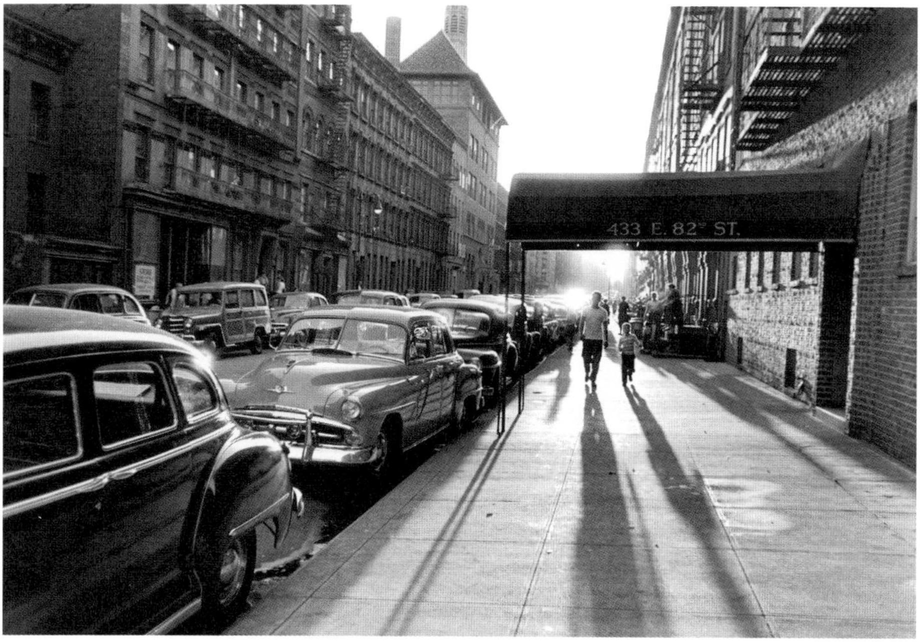

New York, 1953

29 *Monday*

30 *Tuesday*

1 *Wednesday*

2 *Thursday*

3 *Friday*

4 *Saturday*

5 *Sunday*

6 *Monday*

7 *Tuesday*

8 *Wednesday*

9 *Thursday*

10 *Friday*

11 *Saturday*

12 *Sunday*

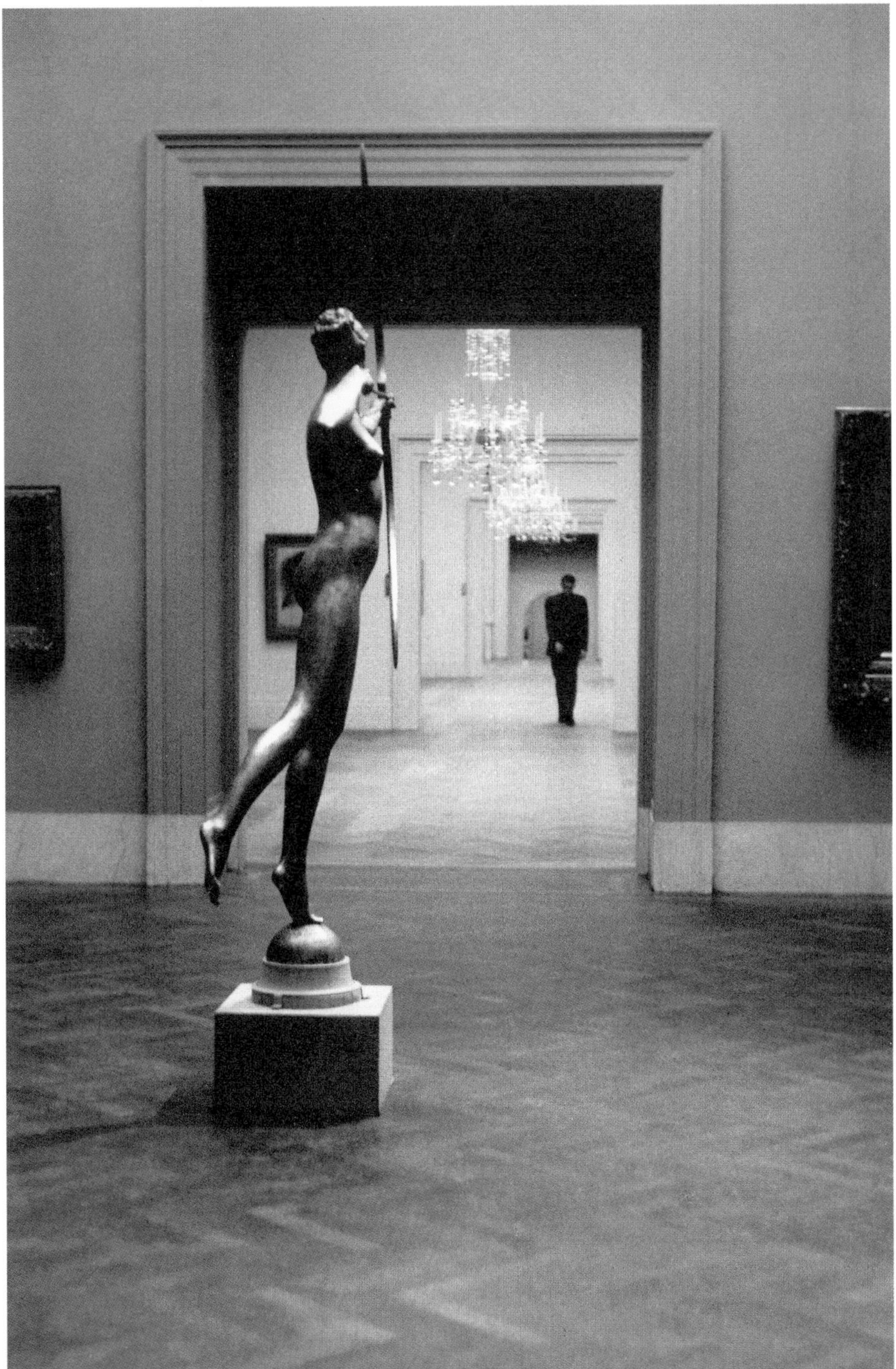

Metropolitan Museum of Art, New York, 1949

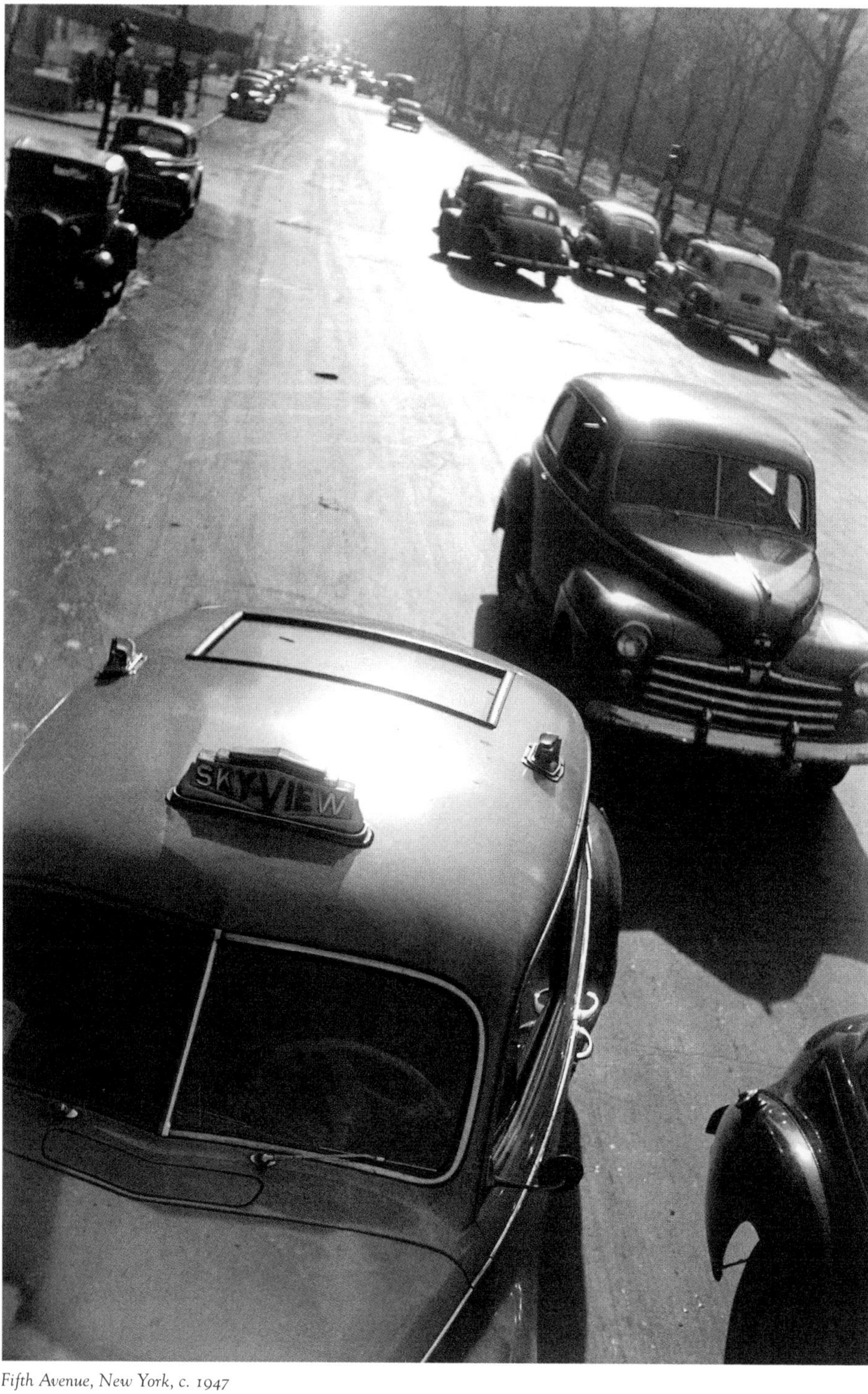

Fifth Avenue, New York, c. 1947

13 Monday

Holiday
(Canada, USA)

14 Tuesday

15 Wednesday

16 Thursday

17 Friday

18 Saturday

19 Sunday

20 *Monday*

21 *Tuesday*

22 *Wednesday*

23 *Thursday*

24 *Friday*

25 *Saturday*

26 *Sunday*

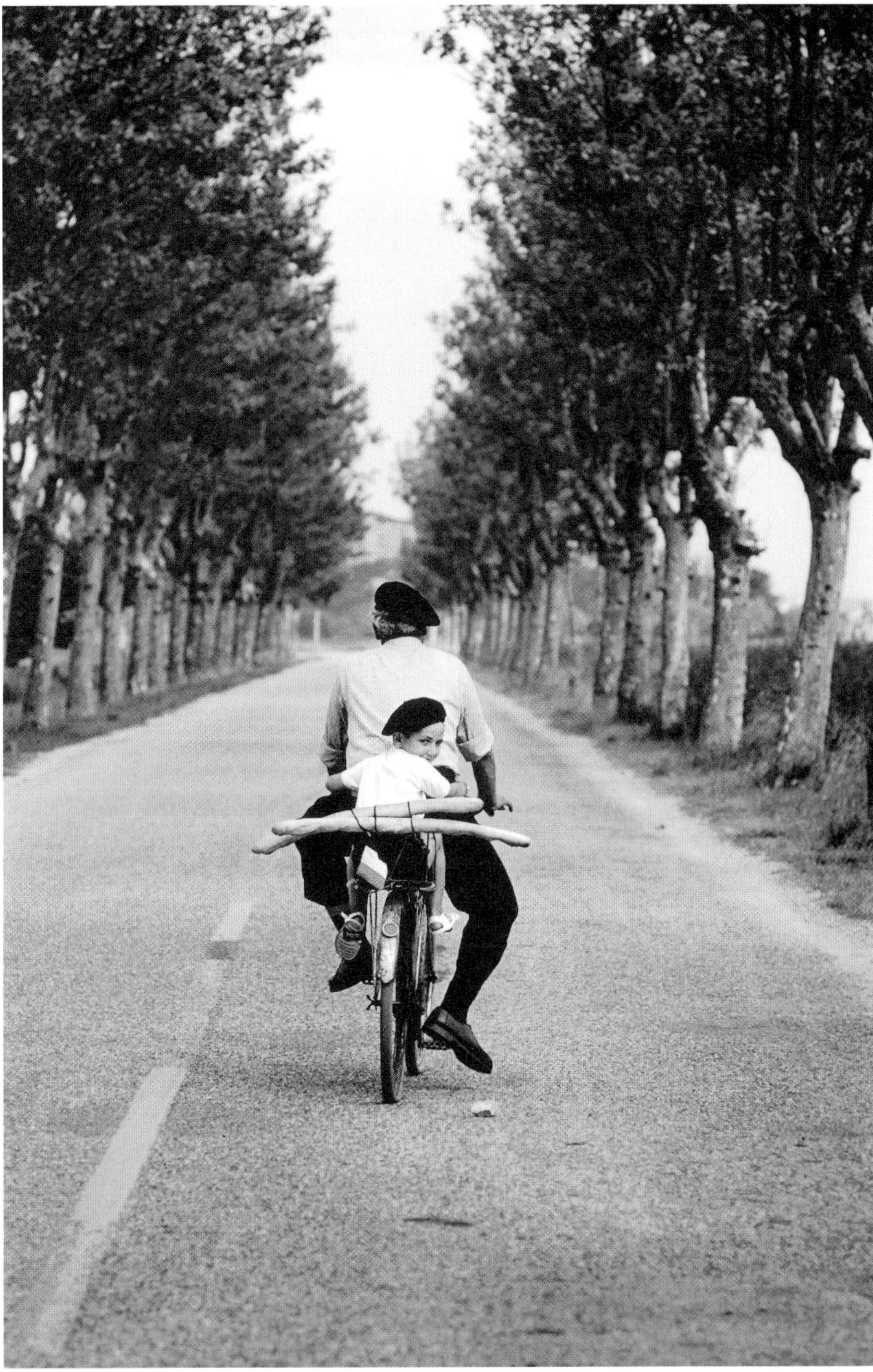

Provence, France, 1955

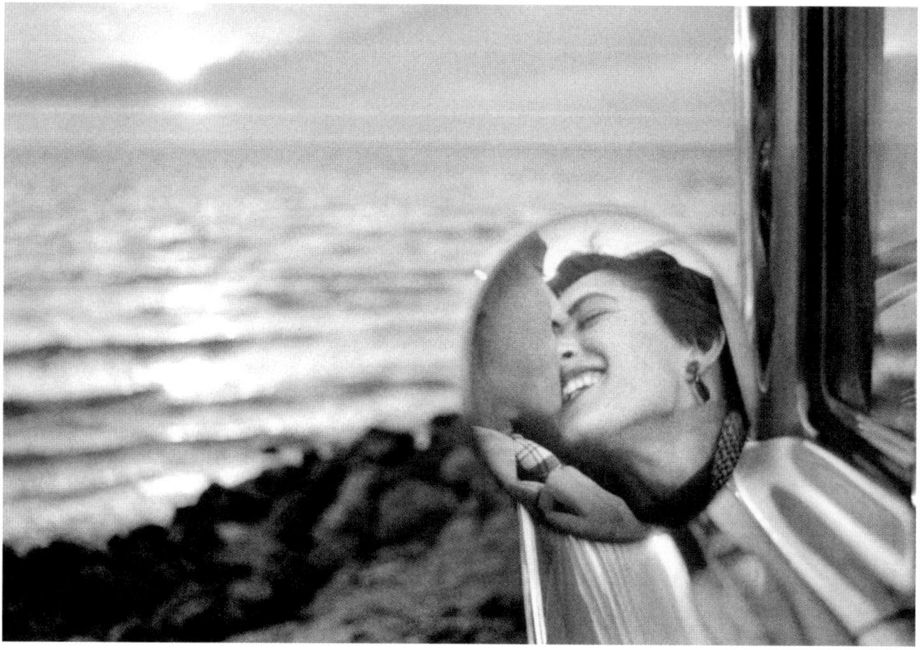

California, 1955

27 Monday

Holiday (New Zealand)

28 Tuesday

29 Wednesday

30 Thursday

31 Friday

1 Saturday

2 Sunday

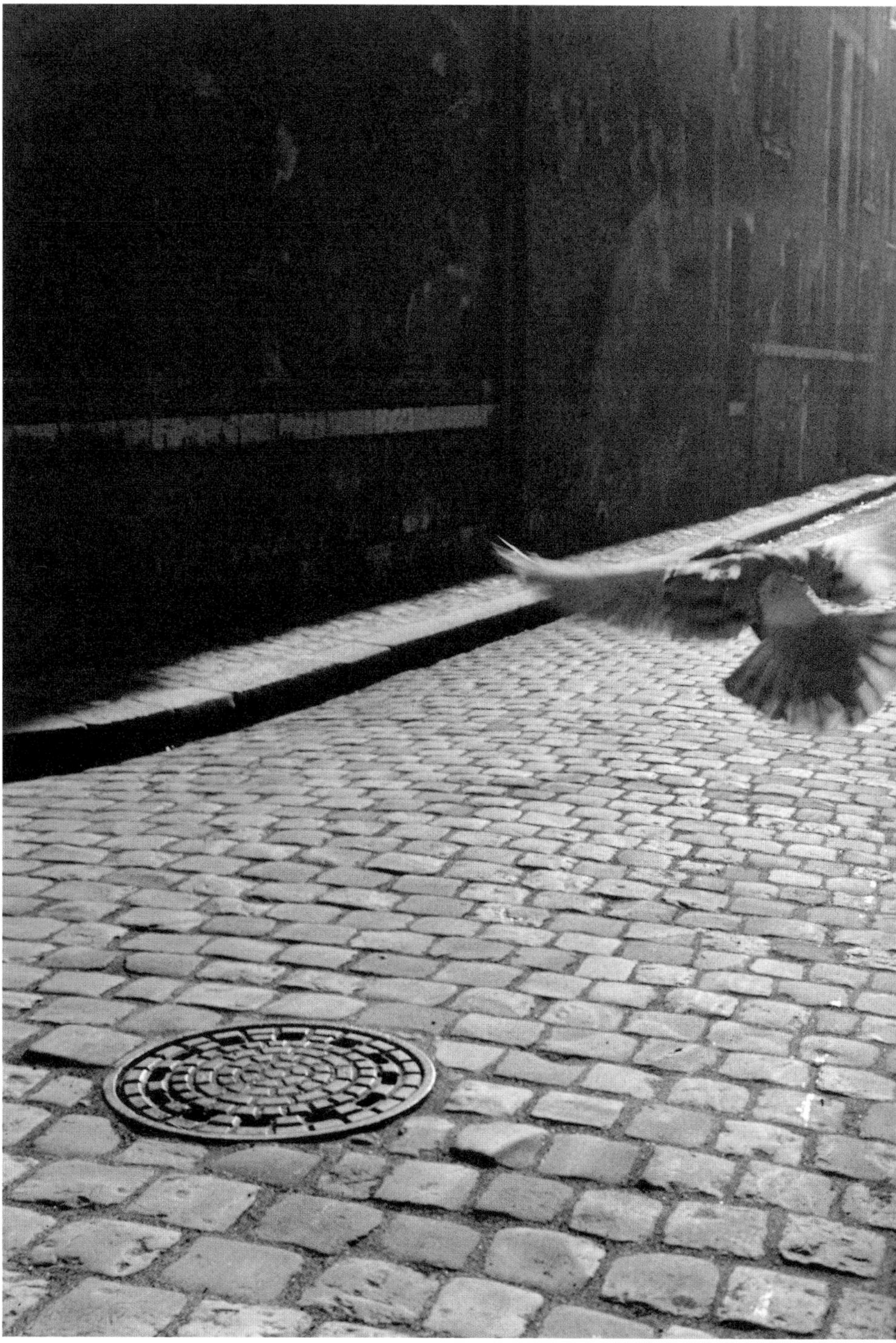

Orléans, France, 1952

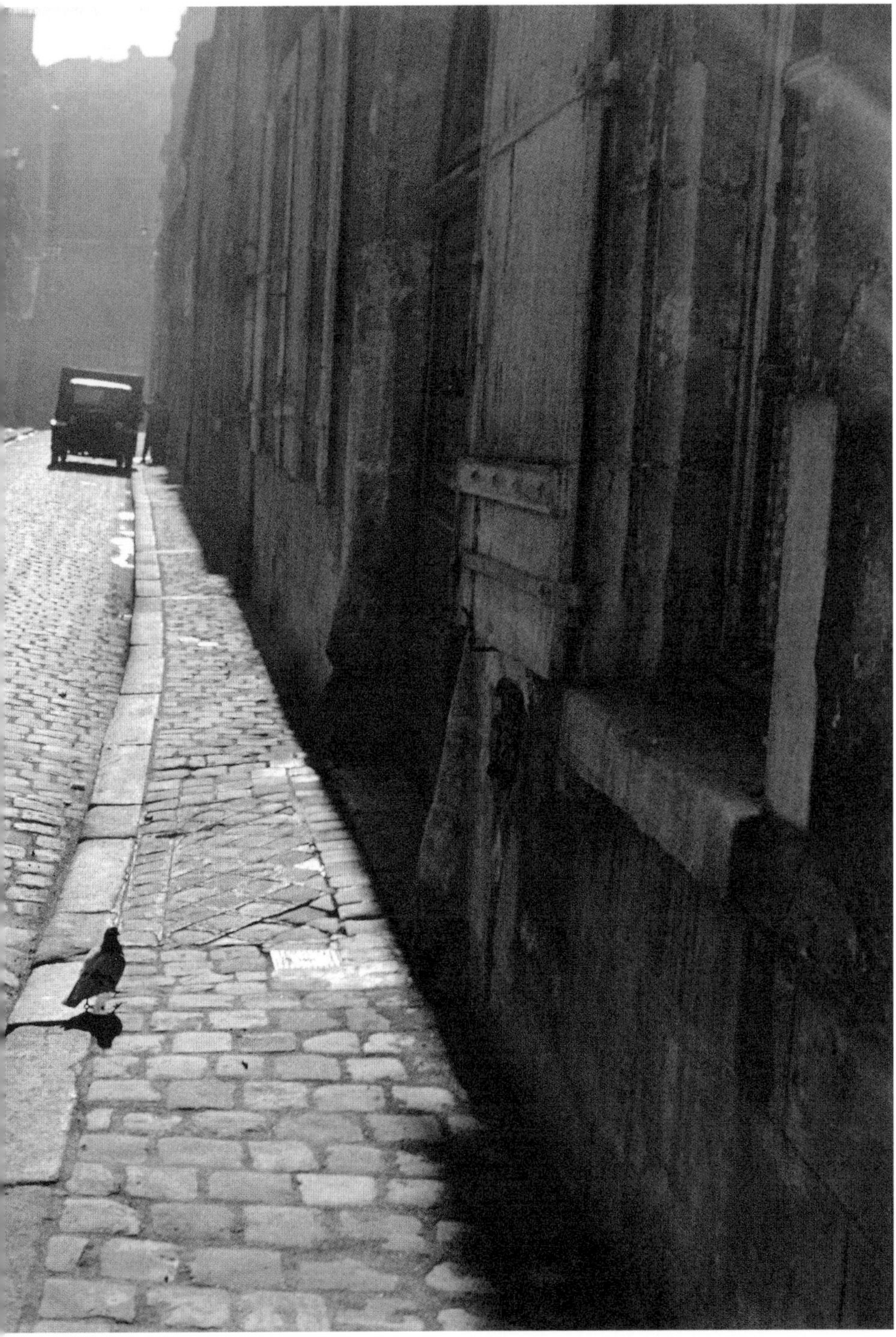

3 *Monday*

4 *Tuesday*

5 *Wednesday*

6 *Thursday*

7 *Friday*

8 *Saturday*

9 *Sunday*

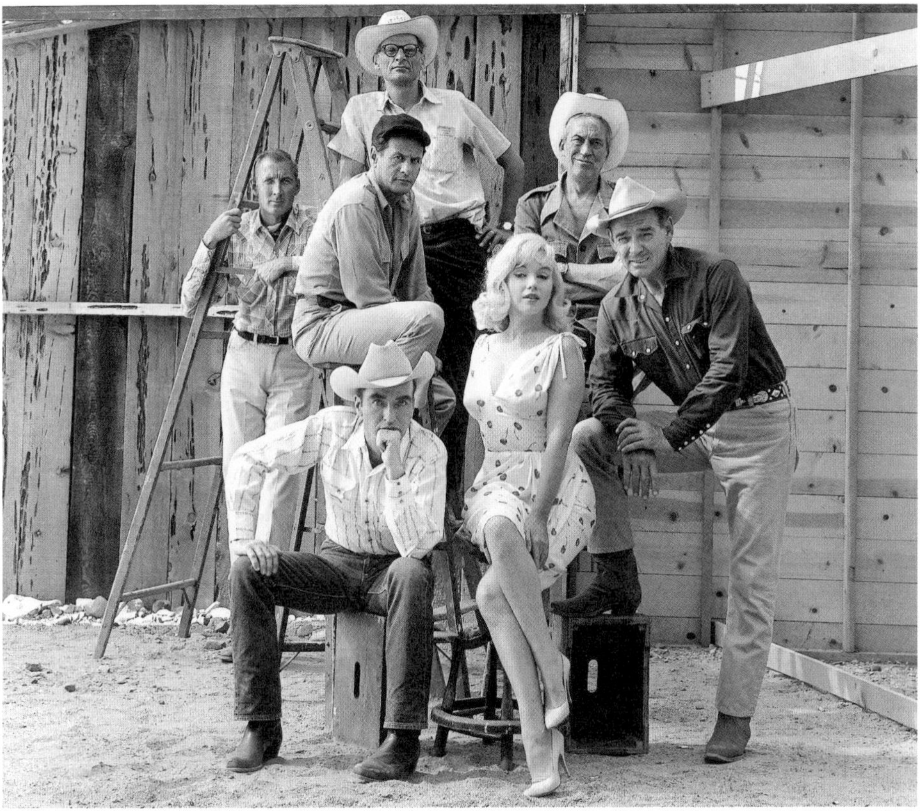

On the set of 'The Misfits', Reno, Nevada, 1960

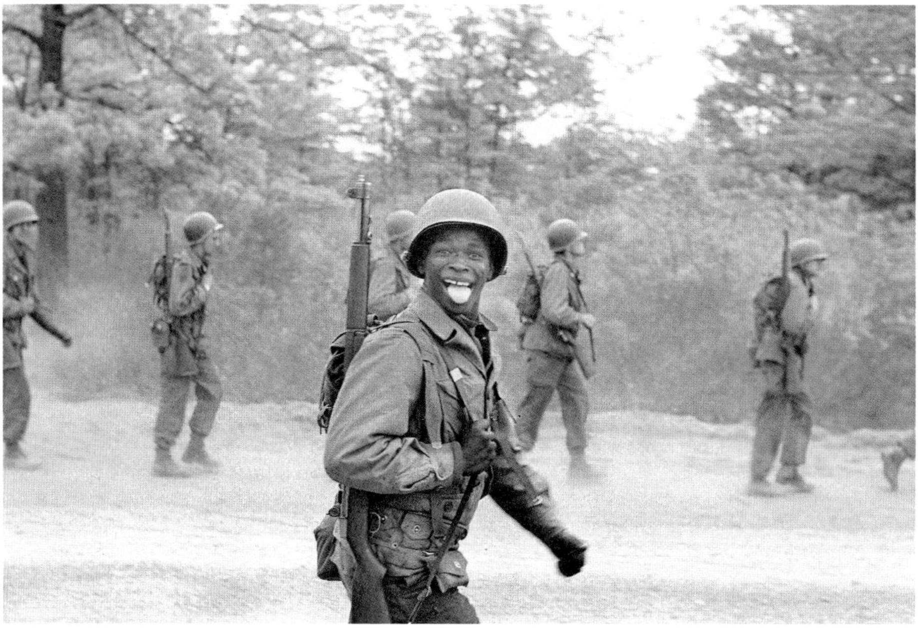

Fort Dix, New Jersey, 1951

10 *Monday*

11 *Tuesday*

Holiday
(Canada, USA)

12 *Wednesday*

13 *Thursday*

14 *Friday*

15 *Saturday*

16 *Sunday*

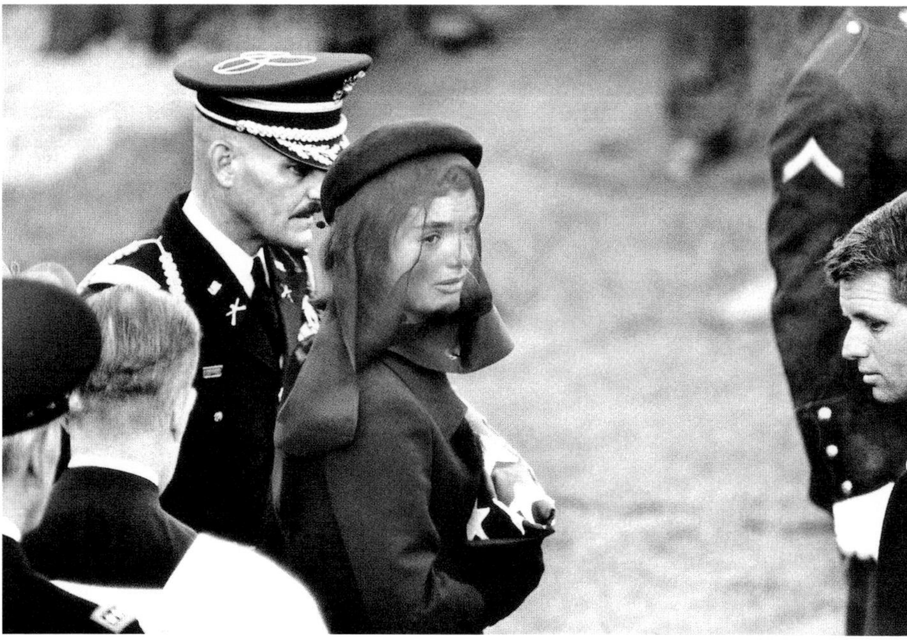

Jackie Kennedy, Arlington, Virginia, 1963

17 *Monday*

18 *Tuesday*

19 *Wednesday*

20 *Thursday*

21 *Friday*

22 *Saturday*

23 *Sunday*

24 Monday

25 Tuesday

26 Wednesday

27 Thursday

Holiday (USA)

28 Friday

29 Saturday

30 Sunday

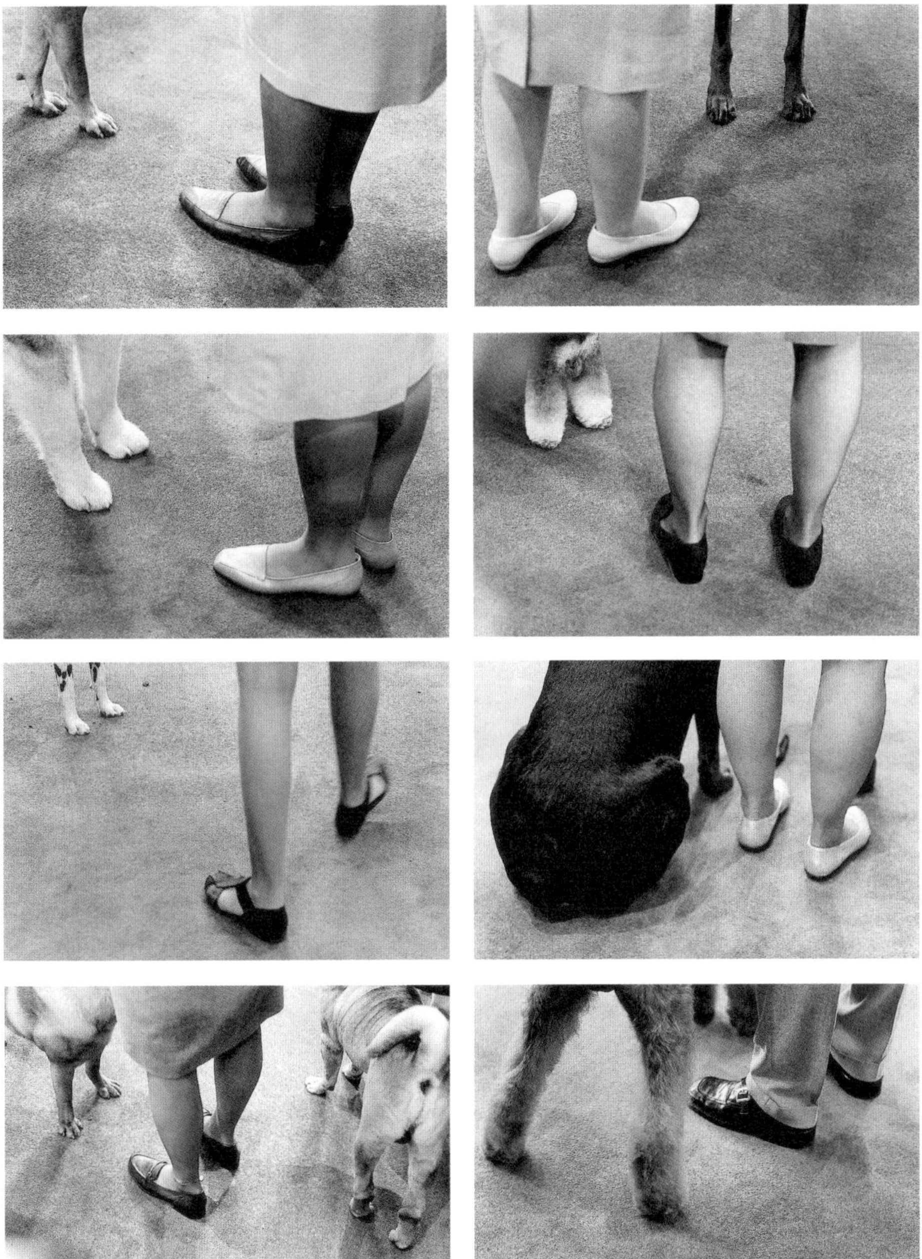

New York, 1999

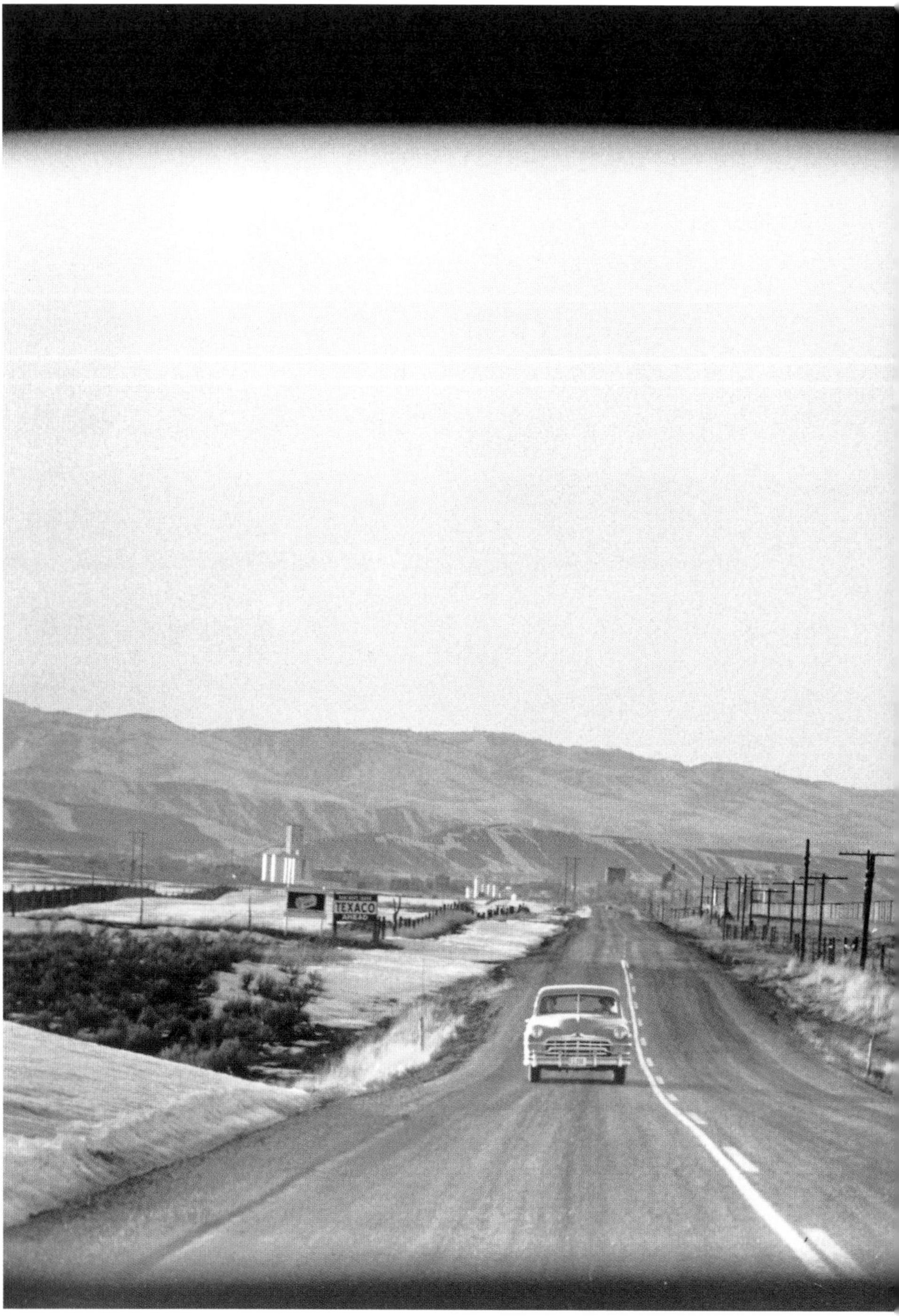

Wyoming, 1954

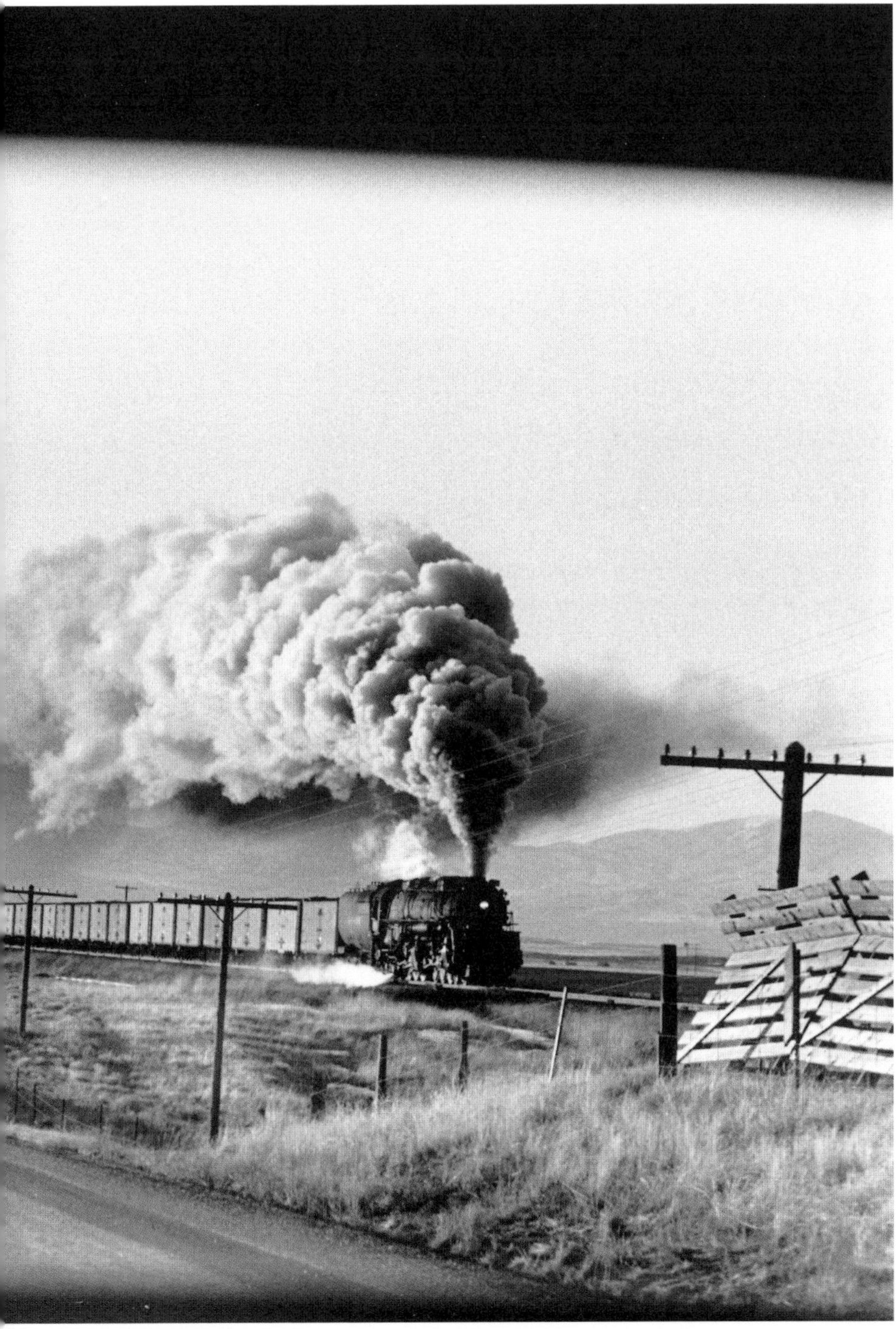

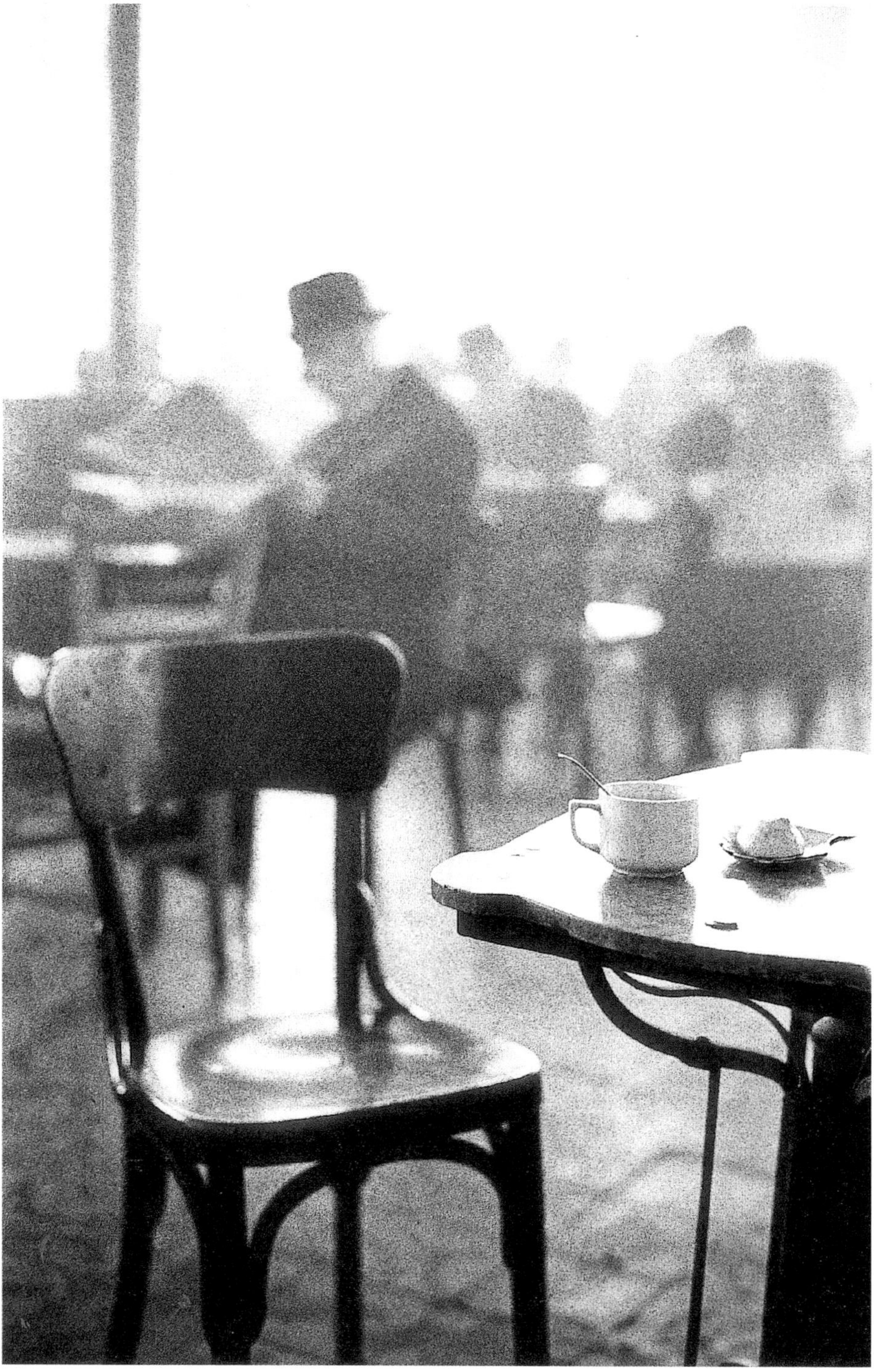

Kalamáta, Greece, 1966

1 *Monday*

2 *Tuesday*

3 *Wednesday*

4 *Thursday*

5 *Friday*

6 *Saturday*

7 *Sunday*

8 *Monday*

9 *Tuesday*

10 *Wednesday*

11 *Thursday*

12 *Friday*

13 *Saturday*

14 *Sunday*

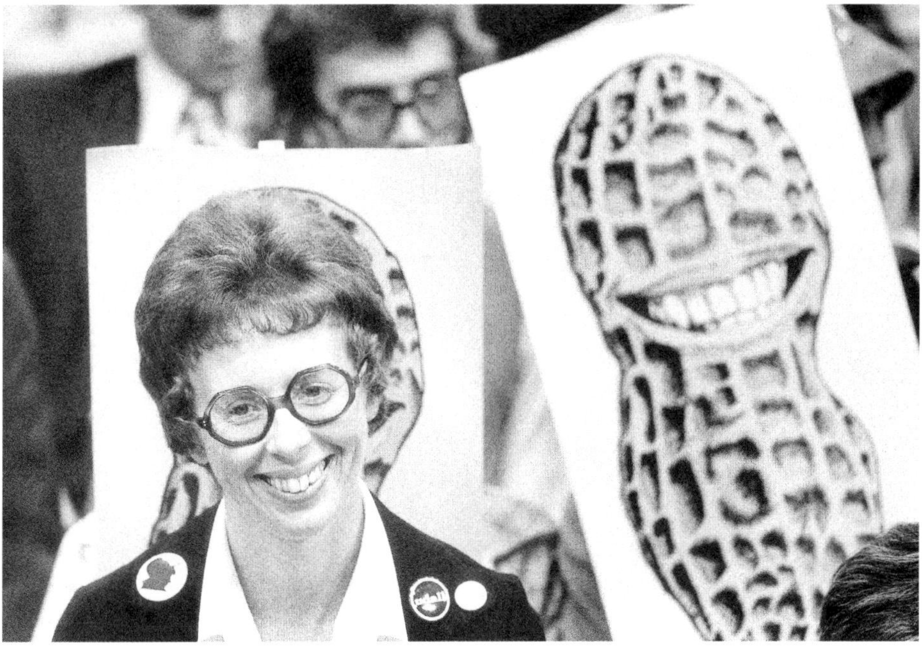

New York, 1976

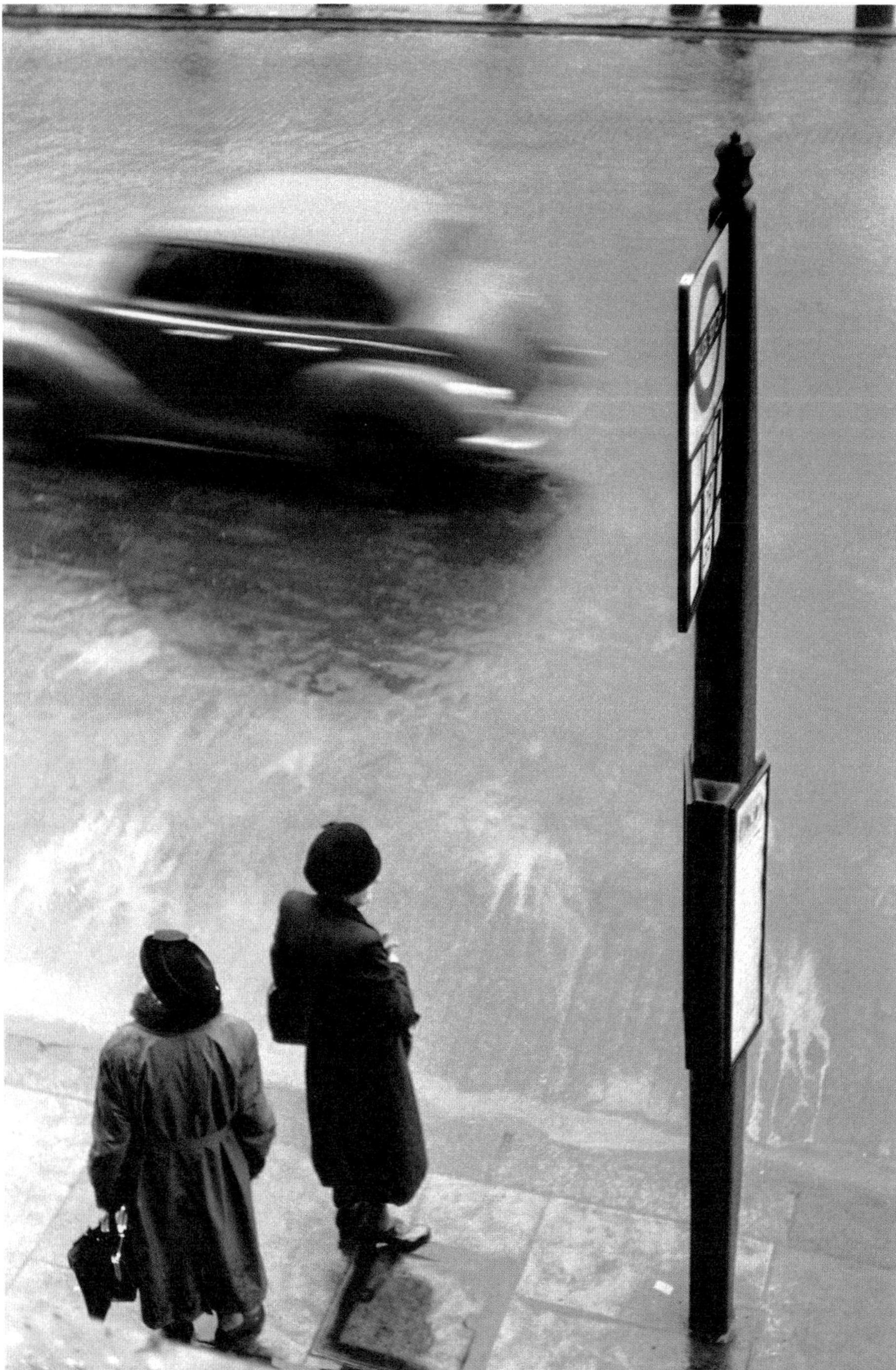

London, 1952

15 *Monday*

16 *Tuesday*

17 *Wednesday*

18 *Thursday*

19 *Friday*

20 *Saturday*

21 *Sunday*

22 *Monday*

23 *Tuesday*

24 *Wednesday*

25 *Thursday*

Holiday

26 *Friday*

Holiday
(UK, Canada, Australia, New Zealand)

27 *Saturday*

28 *Sunday*

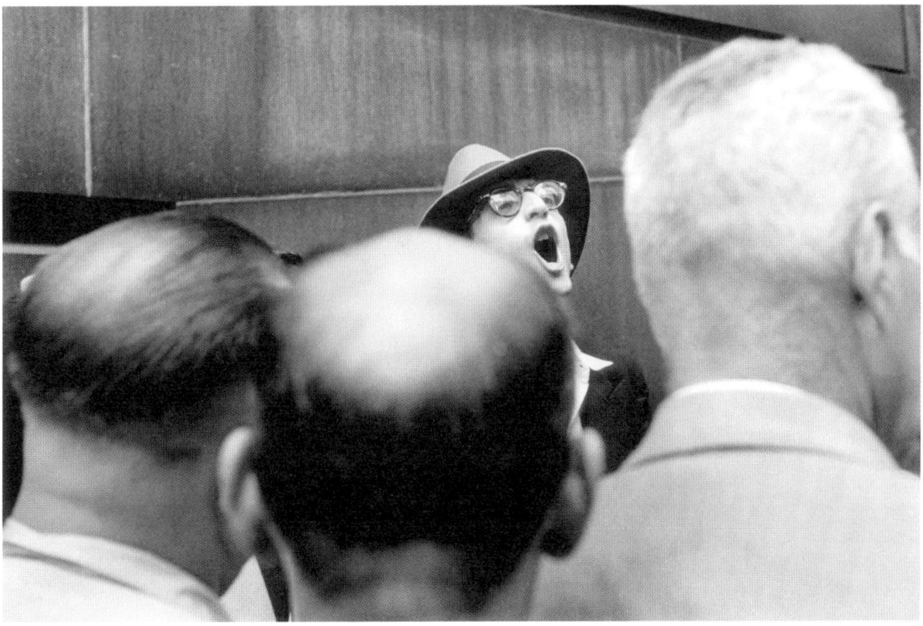

New York, 1955

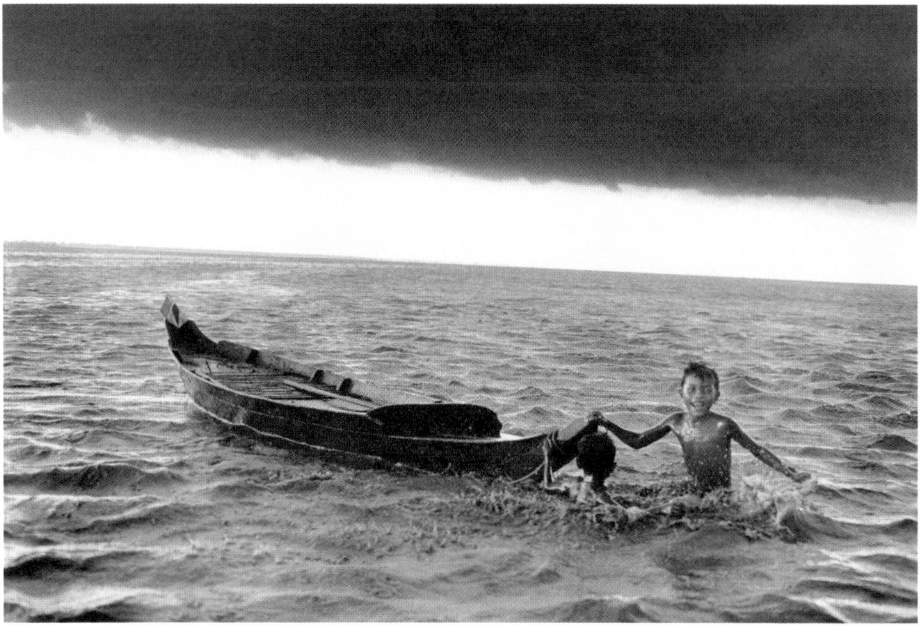

Cambodia, 1998

29 *Monday*

30 *Tuesday*

31 *Wednesday*

1 *Thursday*

2 *Friday*

3 *Saturday*

4 *Sunday*

Phaidon Press Limited
Regent's Wharf
All Saints Street
London N1 9PA

Phaidon Press Inc.
180 Varick Street
New York, NY 10014

www.phaidon.com

First published 2007

Selected from *Elliott Erwitt Snaps*, published by Phaidon Press

Cover illustration: New York, 1953
ISBN-10: 0 7148 4778 X
ISBN-13: 978 0 7148 4778 8

A CIP catalogue record for this book is available from the British Library.

Printed in China